Pamphlet Series of the

Carnegie Endowment for International Peace

Division of International Law

No. 54

THE SPANISH CONCEPTION
OF INTERNATIONAL LAW
AND OF SANCTIONS

BY

JAMES BROWN SCOTT

*Secretary of the Carnegie Endowment for International Peace
and Director of Its Division of International Law;
Professor of International Law, Roman
Law, and Jurisprudence in
Georgetown University*

Reprinted with slight modifications from the
Georgetown Law Journal of January
and March, 1934

WASHINGTON
CARNEGIE ENDOWMENT FOR INTERNATIONAL PEACE
700 JACKSON PLACE, N. W.
1934

PRINTED IN THE UNITED STATES OF AMERICA
AT THE RUMFORD PRESS, CONCORD, N. H.

PREFACE

The present volume contains material originally prepared for delivery as a series of lectures at Georgetown University in commemoration of the three hundredth anniversary of the founding of Maryland. It was printed in the Georgetown Law Journal, and was still later incorporated, in revised form, in *The Catholic Conception of International Law* (Washington, 1934).

The lectures were intended to be an analysis and summary of the conception of the international law with which the Spanish Schoolmen are justly credited. The separate publication of this material is believed to be justified by the fact that they state in brief form the legal and philosophical doctrines, firmly rooted in Christian morality, upon which Francisco de Vitoria and Francisco Suárez founded their modern law of nations.

There are unfortunately no bibliographies devoted to these writers, their period and doctrine. From time to time there have appeared, in foreign languages—notably French and Spanish—certain valuable studies and texts, references to some of which will be found in the footnotes in the following pages. Although in English comparatively little has been done up to the present, mention should be made of the fact that the Carnegie Endowment for International Peace has published in its series of "The Classics of International Law" a volume, *Francisci de Victoria de Indis et de Ivre Belli Relectiones*, edited with an introduction by Ernest Nys, a translation by John Pawley Bate, a reproduction of Simon's edition of Cologne and Frankfort, 1696, and a revised Latin text by Herbert Francis Wright. Volumes containing the portions of Suárez' works which deal with his philosophy of law and of international law are already in manuscript, and will appear in the near future.

Serving as an introduction to the Classics Series, there is in course of publication a detailed study in three parts of "The Spanish Origin of International Law", of which Part I—*Francisco de Vitoria and His Law of Nations*—has already appeared (Oxford, 1933). It contains, in addition to the text proper, translations of the Relectiones *De Indis, De Iure Belli, De Potestate Civili*, and portions of other writings by Victoria. The second and third parts, now in preparation, will analyse, after the method used in the first part, the writings of Suárez, as well as those of Victoria's immediate successors.

October 11–12, 1934.

v

CONTENTS

PART I

FRANCISCO DE VITORIA

VICTORIA'S JUS GENTIUM

The law of nations (*jus gentium*), . . . either is natural law or is derived from natural law (*Inst.*, 1, 2, 1): "What natural reason has established among all nations is called the *jus gentium.*"—*De Indis*, Section III.

If children of any Spaniard be born there [in the New World] and they wish to acquire citizenship, it seems they cannot be barred either from citizenship or from the advantages enjoyed by other citizens—I refer to the case where the parents had their domicile there. The proof of this is furnished by the rule of the law of nations, that he is to be called and is a citizen who is born within the state (*Code*, 7, 62, 11). And the confirmation lies in the fact that, as man is a civil animal, whoever is born in any one state is not a citizen of another state. Therefore, if he were not a citizen of the state referred to, he would not be a citizen of any state, to the prejudice of his rights under both natural law and the law of nations. Aye, and if there be any persons who wish to acquire a domicile in some state of the Indians, as by marriage or in virtue of any other fact whereby other foreigners are wont to become citizens, they can not be impeded any more than others, and consequently they enjoy the privileges of citizens just as others do, provided they also submit to the burdens to which others submit. —*De Indis*, Section III.

And, indeed, there are many things in this connection which issue from the law of nations, which, because it has a sufficient derivation from natural law, is clearly capable of conferring rights and creating obligations. And even if we grant that it is not always derived from natural law, yet there exists clearly enough a consensus of the greater part of the whole world, especially in behalf of the common good of all. For if after the early days of the creation of the world or its recovery from the flood the majority of mankind decided that ambassadors should everywhere be reckoned inviolable and that the sea should be common and that prisoners of war should be made slaves, and if this, namely, that strangers should not be driven out, were deemed a desirable principle, it would certainly have the force of law, even though the rest of mankind objected thereto.—*De Indis*, Section III.

Society could not hold together unless there was somewhere a power and authority to deter wrongdoers and prevent them from injuring the good and innocent. Now, everything needed for the government and the preservation of society exists by natural law, and in no other way can we show that a state has by natural law authority to inflict pains and penalties on its citizens who are dangerous to it. But if a state can do this to its own citizens, society at large no doubt can do it to all wicked and dangerous folk, and this can only be through the instrumentality of princes.—*De Iure Belli*, paragraph 19.

International law has not only the force of a pact and agreement among men, but also the force of a law; for the world as a whole, being in a way one single State, has the power to create laws that are just and fitting for all persons, as are the rules of international law. Consequently, it is clear that they who violate these international rules, whether in peace or in war, commit a mortal sin; moreover, in the gravest matters, such as the inviolability of ambassadors, it is not permissible for one country to refuse to be bound by international law, the latter having been established by the authority of the whole world.—*De Potestate Civili*, Section 21.

PART I

FRANCISCO DE VITORIA'S MODERN LAW OF NATIONS AND ITS MUNICIPAL SANCTIONS

In conformity with the practice of the schoolmen, with at least two of whom I feel almost personally acquainted, and for whose writings I have a profound respect, I propose a text and a thesis. The text is from Francisco de Vitoria's *Relectio De Potestate Civili:* [1]

International law has not only the force of a pact and agreement among men, but also the force of a law; for the world as a whole, being in a way one single State, has the power to create laws that are just and fitting for all persons, as are the rules of international law. Consequently, it is clear that they who violate these international rules, whether in peace or in war, commit a mortal sin; moreover, in the gravest matters, such as the inviolability of ambassadors, it is not permissible for one country to refuse to be bound by international law, the latter having been established by the authority of the whole world.

The thesis is as a corollary from Victoria's [2] text, which is itself a corollary to his Reading *On the Civil Power of the State.*

And the conclusions flowing, as I conceive, from this text are that every rule of international law has a municipal sanction *in esse* or *in posse*, and that a failure to enact a municipal statute for that purpose—or to apply it if enacted—renders the state in default liable in damages.

In 1492, on the 12th day of October, Columbus landed on American soil, of which he took possession in the name of the Spanish sovereigns, and, returning to Spain in the following year, laid a New World at the feet of their Catholic Majesties, Isabella of León and Castile, and Ferdinand of Aragon.

Forty years after the discovery of the New World, a professor of theology in the University of Salamanca, extended to the problems arising through Spanish colonization of the New World the principles of that enlightened justice which the Spanish theologians applied to the relations of the nations and states of Christian civilization.

Thus a Christendom, broken by the Reformation, was replaced by an international community, today universal and embracing all peoples of all continents; the law applicable to members of the Christian community was found to be applicable to non-Christians; and the law of nations, once con-

---

[1] Francisco de Vitoria, *De Potestate Civili*, a *relectio* dated Christmas, 1528. Latin text, Simon's Edition of the *Relectiones Morales*, Cologne and Frankfort (1696), § 21, p. 219 *et seq.* For an English translation of this *Relectio*, see James Brown Scott, *The Spanish Origin of International Law, Part I, Francisco de Vitoria and his Law of Nations* (Oxford, 1934), Appendix C, p. lxxi.

[2] When the full name is used the Spanish form, Francisco de Vitoria, is employed. But when the last name only is given the Latinized (and Englished) form, Victoria, has been adopted as being more familiar to the English-speaking world.

fined to Christendom, has become international. Without ceasing to be Christian in fact, the law of nations became laicized in form; and from century to century it has enlarged its content to meet new conditions by making that express which previously was implicit. Through Francisco de Vitoria it became a science— the science of the rules of social conduct; a moral science, because it applies to moral beings. It was endowed with its philosophy by Francisco Suárez; and it was given its literary form by Grotius in his *Commentary on the Law of Prize*—first written in 1604–5, and revised from time to time, but which unfortunately remained in manuscript until 1868—and its classic and over-elaborated form in his Three Books on the *Law of War and Peace*, published for the first time in 1625, in the midst of a Thirty Years' War.

Thus the discovery of America gave birth to a modern law of nations, Spanish in origin, lay in form, but Catholic in fact and capable of continued development under the control of that Christian morality of which all peoples, and therefore all nations, are the beneficiaries.

The Spanish school came into being and passed out within the course of a century, but it has to its credit the modern law of nations—not merely as law but as a philosophy—Grotius himself saying that "the theologians", and not the professional "jurists", are the ones who "follow natural reason."[1]

Francisco de Vitoria was a Dominican—a member of the Order of Preachers—and he preached to the best of purposes. Before the Society of Jesus came into being, the Dominicans specialized in foreign missions, following in the wake of Columbus, and in this field of beneficent and humanitarian activity Bartolomé Las Casas stands out—and justly—as the Apostle to the Indians, and one whose noble example the Jesuits were later to imitate.

As a Dominican, Victoria was naturally interested in their missions to the New World, which then perhaps loomed larger on the western horizon than now; letters from the brethren beyond the seas passed from hand to hand, and tales of improper conduct on the part of the brethren themselves were not wanting. Victoria's idea was to treat the Indians as brothers and as equals, to help them in their worldly affairs, to instruct them in spiritual matters and lead them to the altar by the persuasion of a Christian life on the part of the missionary. Or, as Chaucer puts it:

> But Cristes lore, and his apostles twelve
> He taught, but first he folwed it himselve.

---

[1] Grotius, *De Iure Praedae*, chapter viii, ms. p. 51: "Qua in parte theologorum magis sententiae, quam iurisperitorum standum est. Illi enim rationem sequuntur naturalem, hi vero instituta civilia, quae utilitatis alicuius causa permittunt fieri saepe, quod alioqui facere non licet."

The manuscript of the *De Iure Praedae*, edited, with an introduction, by H. G. Hamaker, was published at The Hague in 1868 by Martinus Nijhoff. An English translation and a collotype reproduction of the Latin text are now being prepared by the Carnegie Endowment for International Peace and will be published in its series of *The Classics of International Law*.

Deeply versed in the lore of the Church, through his attendance at the University of Paris—then without question the international center—and his contact with thousands of foreigners who, like himself, were completing their studies, lodged in quarters appropriately known as their "nations", and who could not fail to see themselves in their fellow students, it was inevitable that Victoria should make of Aquinas the guide of his life, for St. Thomas was also a Dominican; he also had studied in the University of Paris, and had even been its Rector.   To be sure, the *Sentences* of Peter Lombard were still in vogue, but they were being replaced in matters spiritual by the theology of St. Thomas Aquinas—then and today the doctrine of the Church —and, in matters national and international, by conceptions of St. Thomas, which gave permanent form to the views of Aristotle on the nature of the state, and to the views of St. Augustine on the two great questions which interest and baffle us today—war and peace.

When Victoria became *prima* professor of theology in Salamanca in 1526, the conceptions of St. Thomas also made their appearance, and when Victoria died twenty years later, the doctrine, spiritual and temporal, of St. Thomas remained as a monument of Victoria's foresight and influence.

When in 1532 Victoria prepared his public Reading *On the Indians Lately Discovered*,[1] he appropriately preferred the Old to the New Testament, for was not his text—"Teach all nations, baptizing them in the name of the Father, and of the Son and of the Holy Spirit."   The text involved the baptism of children of tender age, of unbelievers, without the consent of their parents.   The authorities which he invoked were Peter Lombard and of course St. Thomas Aquinas, Doctors of the Church—the *Sententiae* (Dist. 4) of the former, and the *Secunda Secundae* (Question 10, Art. 12), and the *Tertia Pars* (Question 68, Art. 10), of the latter.   Here a casual reader turning the page might perhaps lay the Reading aside without troubling himself further with Victoria, his text or his authorities; but if he were a Spaniard, the next sentence would hold him spellbound as Coleridge's Ancient Mariner held the unwilling wedding guest.

"The whole of this controversy and discussion," Victoria declares, "was started on account of the aborigines of the New World, commonly called Indians, who came forty years ago into the power of the Spaniards, not having been previously known to our world."   Here we have Victoria's own statement that the controversy of which he was to discourse had arisen not

[1] For a scholarly reproduction of the first and second editions of Victoria's *Relectiones* (Lyons, 1557, and Salamanca, 1565) as well as of the manuscripts of the *Relectiones* as taken down by Victoria's students, see the first volume of the *Relecciones Teológicas del Maestro Fray Francisco de Vitoria*, edited by P. Mtro. Fr. Luis G. Alonso Getino (Madrid, 1933). A second volume, which has just been issued, contains a critical edition of several of Victoria's readings, together with an admirable Spanish translation.

For a reproduction of the Simon edition (1696) of two of Victoria's *Relectiones, De Indis Recenter Inventis* and *De Jure Belli*, together with a translation, see the volume *De Indis et De Jure Belli Relectiones*, published by the Carnegie Institution of Washington in 1917, in the Series of *The Classics of International Law*.   This volume contains an introduction by Ernest Nys, a translation of the text by John Pawley Bate, and a revised text by Herbert Francis Wright.   For the reproduction of *De Indis* see p. 302 and for the translation, p. 45.

merely on account of the discovery of the New World, but because of the Indians coming into the power of the Spaniards. There is power and there is power. There is the power of justice; there is, unfortunately, the power of injustice. The question which confronted and deeply concerned Victoria, who insisted that the conduct of his government should be right, and that the duty of right-minded men was to set it aright—or at least endeavor to do so—was whether the Spaniards, his countrymen, were justified in taking possession of the territories of the aborigines of the New World, commonly called Indians, and, if so, on what grounds; if not—to use an academic expression—why not? And the question being one of right, which may be and often is different from law—since the conventional view is that right is a moral, whereas law is a legal conception—caused Victoria to state that "it is not for jurists to settle this question or at any rate not for jurists only," for "since the barbarians in question . . . were not in subjection by human law; it is not by human, but by divine law that questions concerning them are to be determined." Why was this so? Because, Victoria adds, and very properly, in terms applicable to our day as well: "Jurists are not skilled enough in the divine law to be able by themselves to settle questions of this sort"; nor was he sure that "in the discussion and determination of this question theologians have ever been called competent to pronounce on so grave a matter." Why was the matter so grave? "And as the issue," he continued, "concerns the forum of conscience, its settlement belongs to the priests, that is, to the Church."

We have just referred to the conventional view that law and right may differ, that the legal conception and the moral conception are things apart. But is this true? Are not the two sets of terms, in fact, complementary? What is morality without rules? And what is law without the moral guide of justice? If we insist that law be moral, instead of a mere command of an artificial superior, then we shall make morality the test of law and find ourselves in accord with Victoria and the Spanish School.

But Victoria had in mind an additional purpose, which he reveals by asking: "In order that the whole of the matter be adequately examined and assured, is it not possible that so weighty a business may produce other special doubts deserving of discussion?" He answered that he thought that he would be "doing something which is not only not futile and useless, but well worth the trouble, if"—speaking in the first person—"I am enabled to discuss this question in a manner befitting its importance." He did discuss, in its various aspects, this international event which, in its material aspect, is supposed to be the most important event of modern history—indeed, it separates the medieval from the modern world. And the discussion, conducted "in a manner befitting its importance," was not only "not futile and useless, but well worth the trouble," as it resulted in the modern law of nations, which is also, in no slight degree, the law of nations of the future.

To come, however, to the opening paragraph of Victoria's Reading *On the Indians Lately Discovered*. The "disputation about them" was to fall into three parts. It did. In the first he inquired "by what right these Indian natives came under Spanish sway." This phase of the subject required an examination not merely from the national but from the international point of view, leading him to state those principles of right and wrong in international relations, which he himself, as a high-minded son of the Church, with a legal training as sound as his conception of morality, considered applicable.

But the question was even larger, for the second part dealt with the rights which "the Spanish sovereigns obtained over them"—the Indians recently discovered—"in temporal and civil matters", these rights, of course, to be tested by right, not might. But the question was even broader than this, involving not only the rights of the sovereigns, but those which "the Church obtained over them"—meaning, of course, the American barbarians—"in matters spiritual and touching religion." These questions required an answer equally broad in scope—an answer involving the law of international relations: the right of a foreign nation to impose itself on equals as well as on inferior nations; and also the spiritual relations of nations and their peoples to one another. Under three headings we have the program of the modern international law.

As the relations of the Spaniards and the Indians were relations, to use Victoria's own phrase, "of Indian principalities" with the Spanish monarch —in other words, relations of state with state—it is not merely advisable, but essential that we consider the state, its origin and its purpose, from within, before proceeding to its external relations and discussing whether, either as a mere state, or as a single state in an association of states, it possesses a municipal sanction, *in esse* or *in posse*, for every rule of the law of nations.

Victoria, as we have said, was elected *prima* professor of theology in the University of Salamanca in 1526, having been previously appointed professor and also director of studies in the University of Vallodolid, in the then capital of Spain. The method at that time of choosing a professor was interesting and bids fair to make its appearance again—that is, a competition with public disquisitions of the candidates upon set subjects, in the presence of the students, who would choose from among the candidates for the chair the one who seemed best to meet requirements. Assuredly in Victoria's case the choice has met with the approval of succeeding centuries. It gave him the opportunity which he no doubt had in mind, since his eighteen years in France in the formative period of his life had confirmed him in internationalism—for who, belonging to a church which was international, could help but be an internationalist?

Now there were two professors of theology in the University of Salamanca—the *prima* and the *vespera*—the holder of the *prima* chair—the more coveted—meeting his class at six o'clock in the morning, when the student body was not worn out by the day's task, as was probably the case when its

members came together at vespers in the afternoon.   Probably also that was
the reason why the morning class was but an hour and a half in duration,
whereas in the afternoon it sat in continuous session at the feet of the *vespera*
master for two full hours.   The later period seems to us more attractive,
although perhaps early or late Victoria would draw today as he did at Salamanca, where his auditors were said to number a round thousand.

It was the duty of the *prima* professor, in addition to his teaching, to
deliver at least once a year a public address or disquisition, ordinarily based
upon the course which he had professed throughout an academic term.   The
course consisted of *lectiones* or daily readings and the *publicum* (the term in
vogue in Germany) was called a *relectio*, which would be considered not as a
re-reading of the entire course but as a re-statement of the views which had
been set forth more at length.

As the international law of Victoria, as well as of other persons learned in
the subject, is the law applicable to states and their peoples, it is necessary
to discuss in some detail Victoria's conception of the origin and nature of the
state and its government.   And as a prelude to this discussion it will be
advisable to give an outline of his conception in summary form.   Victoria's
view on the origin and nature of the state is the Aristotelian view that man,
as a social and political animal, must live in organized society; and this,
Victoria holds, by both divine and natural law.   There must be government,
for the people would fall apart if the rights of each were not accompanied by
the correlative duties.   In this government the source of power is twofold.
It is divine, in that, according to a text adopted by Victoria, "all power is
from God"; and it is human in that the form and exercise of that power
depend upon the will of the majority of the people.

The introductory remarks to Victoria's *Relectio* on the State (*De Potestate
Civili*) [1] are in the nature of a justification, not merely of the topic which he
had chosen, but of the method of its presentation.   In the words of Victoria .

The duties and functions of the theologian extend over a field so vast, that no argument,
no discussion, no text, seem alien to the practice and purpose of theology.   And this may
account for the fact that the lack of able and sound theologians is as great as—not to say
greater than—the lack of orators which is mentioned by Cicero, and which he explains by
saying that men who are distinguished and skilled in every science and in all the arts are
very rare.   Theology, indeed, is the first of all those sciences and studies which the Greeks
call θεολογία.

Consequently, there is no occasion for surprise, if very few are found who are competent
in a subject so difficult.   In this immense domain, then, and in the extensive field composed
of the writings of all scholars, an infinite number of possibilities present themselves; but I
have selected one passage for special notice: surely if it merits my consideration and treatment of it, it is worthy—most illustrious and learned gentlemen—of your attention.   The
passage, then, concerns the State: a matter with regard to which many points remain to be
considered, although earnest and erudite men have already accorded it extensive treatment.
Since the topic is too broad to be disposed of in a single discussion, I have chosen as the subject for today the public and private power by which States are governed.

[1] See *supra*, p. 1, note 1.

The passage to be read and commented upon is from the 'Master of the Sentences' (2d. 44), and is based upon the words of Paul (*Romans* 13:1): 'There is no power but of God.' Although a multitude of topics might be brought up in connection with this passage, nevertheless, our entire discussion shall be limited for the present to laic or secular power, in order that we may not be more discursive and rambling than is needful.

Victoria was not merely a master of the scholastic method, but through him the old scholastic method was renewed so as to apply to the newer theology whereof he was also the accredited master. The favorite authorities of Victoria's day in matters of the state were Aristotle and Cicero, and through Victoria we hear, as it were, their voices. As a Christian the New Testament was his guide, and just as in the case of the Reading *On the Indians Lately Discovered*, he took his text, in the Reading *On the Civil Power*, from the *Sentences* of Peter Lombard, from St. Augustine and from the *Summa* of St. Thomas Aquinas.

But to the state. The first question which confronted Victoria was the source of power; and the power "by which the secular State is governed"— the words are those of Victoria, for his concern was the secular state—"is not only just and legitimate, but is so surely ordained of God, that not even by the consent of the whole world can it be destroyed or annulled."

Now power, he says, "is twofold—public and private"—and Victoria's first anxiety was to state "the causes of civil laic power," as it was to be, he says, "the subject of the whole lecture." He here invokes the authority of Aristotle, to the effect that "'necessity' should be considered from the viewpoint of purpose," the first, as Aristotle holds, "of all causes, and the principal one."

What, then, of "the purpose that underlies the establishment of the power which we are about to consider?" Mother Nature looked after the animal world, supplying it with the means of protection. "To man alone," Victoria says, "she granted reason and virtue," and man being endowed with reason, could not live in solitude, either for his own comfort or for the perpetuation of the species; and he was likewise endowed with speech, "the messenger of the understanding," inasmuch as, in the famous phrase of Aristotle, he is a civil and sociable animal. For justice—"and the same is true of friendship"—cannot be "practised except by the multitude" (to be understood in this connection as meaning, it is believed, "more than one").

"Therefore," says Victoria, "since human societies have been established for this purpose—namely, that we should bear one another's burdens—and civil society is of all societies that which best provides for the needs of men, it follows that the community is, so to speak, an exceedingly natural form of inter-communication."

But "a single family is not self-sufficing." If society is in accord with nature, then it follows that states and commonwealths are not the invention of man, but of nature, "who produced this method of protecting and preserving mortals."

What is the conclusion which Victoria draws from these premises? That "the same purpose and necessity underlie the existence of public powers," and that hence, public powers are in accord with nature, and therefore "the use and the utility of public power, and of the community, and of society are absolutely the same." Why this identity? "For if all were equal," Victoria says, "and subject to no power, each individual would draw away from the others in accordance with his own opinions and will." What would be the consequence? "The commonwealth would of necessity be torn apart; and the State would be dissolved."

These observations are of the utmost importance, lying as they do at the root of government. Victoria was apparently of this opinion, because he invoked the authority of the New Testament, contained in substantially the same wording in three of the Gospels: "Every kingdom divided against itself shall be brought to desolation"; and "where there is no ruler . . . the people shall perish." The conclusion of Victoria on this phase of the subject is that "if States and societies are established in accordance with divine or natural law, the same is true of power, without which States could not exist." This is design in nature, according to the Greeks; according to the Christians, God in action.

In the Victorian conception, government must be according to the law natural and divine, but the form of the government must depend upon the state, that is, the people united in a community, "which by its very nature is competent to govern and administer itself, and to order all its powers for the common good." In this connection, Victoria reverts to the statement he has already made—that if the state were without a head, "the commonwealth would of necessity be torn apart," to use again his language. For if all were equal, there would be no superior, and consequently in an assembly no "one individual" could of himself assume authority, "in view of the fact that every man has by natural law the power and the right to defend himself, there being nothing more natural than to repel force by force." But if the state were not, so to speak, "beheaded," the situation would be otherwise, since the community or state might protect the right of each individual, "in order to preserve the integrity of the whole, and in a spirit of devotion to the public good."

What should be the governing will—that of a single person—as in a monarchy (which Victoria prefers); or should authority be vested in a select few (as in an aristocracy); or vested in the many (as in the case of a democracy)? We of today must supply our own answer to this question.

But whatever the form, it is necessary that the administration of the state should be entrusted to the care of some person or persons (and it matters not whether this power is entrusted to one or to many). If this were not so, Victoria would be sore pressed to acknowledge that "princes and other magistrates found among pagans are legitimate."

What, then, is the Victorian definition of public secular power? It is

"the faculty, authority, or right to govern the civil State," whether it be Christian or pagan; but be the government a monarchy, an aristocracy, or a democracy there need be no less liberty in one than in another, and the ruler of one or the other binds the state, which "as a whole may rightfully be punished for the sin of the monarch"—meaning thereby the chief executive. To such an extent is this true that, in Victoria's words, "if any king make unjust war upon another ruler, the injured party may plunder and make lawful war upon and slay the subjects of the unjust king, even if all these subjects be innocent; for when the king"—or other agency—"has once been set up by the State, any immoderate act of his is charged against the State."

That the head of the state—whatever the name, whether consisting of one or of a number—is to be chosen by a majority of the people, and is to be subject to the government which has been established, is clear from the illustrations which Victoria gives. "Just as the majority of members of a State may set up a king over the whole State, although other members are unwilling," so "in free States such as Venice and Florence, the majority may elect a king even though the rest of the citizens be opposed." The proof in either case betrays a subtlety on the part of the great Dominican which would seem to be more natural to Suárez than to Victoria. "It suffices," Victoria says, "in order to do anything legitimately, that the majority should agree on the course in question." "This point," he observes, much to our pleasure, "can be satisfactorily demonstrated," adding by way of illustration: "For if two parties disagree, it must necessarily result that the sentiment of one party should prevail; and inasmuch as their desires conflict, the sentiment of the party which is in the minority ought not to prevail; therefore it is the sentiment of the majority which should dominate." Victoria, although not given to hairsplitting, as is the wont of the philosopher, adds: "If the consent of all is required in order to create the king, why is it not also required in order that he be not so created? Why is unanimous consent more to be required in an affirmative than in a negative matter?"—a doctrine which applies, it would seem, in the unmaking as well as in the making of an agent of the state.

The dethroning of a monarch is thus the prerogative of the majority, and a revolt is justifiable if only it has the support of the majority in its behalf.

In short, governments are made by peoples, not by princes. The state has the power of self-government, as in the case of the Venice and Florence of Victoria's day—not to speak of this Western World of ours; "for the State," he says, "has the power of self-government, and the act of the greater part is the act of the whole; therefore, the State may accept the form of government that it desires, even if this be not the best form. Rome, for example, possessed an aristocratic government, which is not the best type." In this we agree, preferring a representative democracy.

At the beginning of his public address *On the Civil Power*, Victoria stated that the Reading would be restricted to certain conclusions. Having dis-

posed of various preliminary matters, he devotes the balance of the Reading to a final and all important conclusion: "the laws and constitutions of princes are binding in such a way as to render transgressors guilty in the court of conscience." This is indeed a weighty subject, about which there was a difference of opinion. The importance of the conclusion was not lost upon Victoria; otherwise he would not have assigned it, as it were, the place of honor. "If time permitted," he said, "many points neither futile nor unworthy of mention might be brought up in this connection and in support of this conclusion. But inasmuch as a lengthy discussion would be inopportune," doubtless out of consideration for his audience, "I shall dispose of the whole matter in as few words as possible." We shall follow his example. First he stated the view of his opponents, who held that "the laws possess no force which renders transgressors guilty in the court of conscience," admitting, however, that "princes and magistrates may justly punish the violators of said laws." The concession in this matter is immaterial, inasmuch as the violations of the laws of the state are punishable by the appropriate authorities of the state.

However, it seemed to Victoria "indubitable that civil laws are binding in the court of conscience." His authority? The Apostle Paul: "Wherefore ye must needs be subject, not only for wrath, but also for conscience sake." [1] Victoria adds: "And Peter[2] says: 'Submit yourselves to every ordinance of man for the Lord's sake: whether it be to the king, as supreme . . .', an admonition," Victoria adds, "which would seem entirely unintelligible if laws were binding only in the courts of civil contentions and not in the court of conscience." Victoria then says "that civil laws are binding under pain of sin and guilt, in the same manner as ecclesiastical laws."

The two kinds of law he finds in agreement, for "divine law so endows a thing with the quality of a virtue or a vice that anything which is in accordance with the mandates of divine laws is rendered good and serviceable, although it would not otherwise be possessed of these characteristics; whereas that which is prohibited by divine law has in it something evil and vicious which it would not otherwise have."

A little later he adds: "In like manner, human law has this same power to endow anything with the quality of a virtue, and its opposite with the quality of a vice." Therefore he states his opinion in two short sentences: "There is no difference in this respect between human and divine law. For in both cases, just as there is merit in an act of virtue, so guilt attends a vicious act."

The violation of divine laws is a mortal, not a venial, sin. To the objection that the human law does not state whether the violation is a mortal or a venial sin, Victoria answers that "not even in divine law, and especially not in natural law, is a statement always included as to whether a given precept concerns mortal or venial sin." In each case, the question of mortal or

---

[1] *Romans*, xiii. 5.　　　　[2] *I Peter*, ii. 13.

venial sin "must be decided according to the particular case involved." Perhaps even today it is not superfluous to add that taxation is necessary for the well-being of the state. Victoria says roundly indeed, that "if any one should fail to pay his taxes, he would be committing a mortal sin," and among other illustrations he more than intimates that "if it is prohibited that any one should carry money out of the country, all those who do so are committing a mortal sin," from which it appears that Victoria was a man of the world as well as a theologian.

There are two questions of more than passing importance which Victoria discusses and which have greatly perplexed the past: "Has the king power to exempt one from liability to guilt, if he should so desire"—meaning, may the king, or, as we would say, the chief executive, issue a pardon of an offense and remit a punishment? His answer is "that without doubt he is empowered to do so." This power of exemption, after trial and conviction, is universally conceded, although it should be and is only sparingly used. The next question is whether the laws of the state are binding upon the members of the legislature who enact them and upon kings—meaning, of course, chief executives as well. There was a difference of opinion on this matter in his time, and it was that difference of opinion in the English-speaking world which brought the head of Charles Stewart to the block. Victoria was clear about the matter, maintaining against opposition that both legislators and executives are bound—for a reason which is worth while noting: "although the act of creating the law be voluntary on the part of the king; nevertheless, the fact that he is thereby bound or not bound, does not depend upon his own will: just as in the case of pacts; for he who enters into a pact of his own free will, is nevertheless bound thereby."

The assimilation of a pact to a law, binding those who have entered into it voluntarily, can not be passed over, for, although Victoria is dealing with the state—that is, men, women and children in association, and therefore forming a society—he had also in mind the association of the states and their peoples in a larger community extending beyond the narrow confines of Europe and embracing in our day the entire world, which society, being composed of natural persons, would disintegrate and the association dissolve, if, although equal, its members did not vest their governments with authority to make laws, to compel their execution and to punish their violation. So also the larger community composed of these states would fall asunder, if there were not laws, and pacts having the force of laws, whereby the states forming the international community should conform their actions to the laws and pacts of their making. Therefore, to quote again Victoria's conclusion in his own language, as it was and still is the goal toward which the forward-looking and far-seeing are directed:

From all that has been said, a corollary may be inferred, namely: that international law has not only the force of a pact and agreement among men, but also the force of a law; for the world as a whole, being in a way one single State, has the power to create laws that are just

and fitting for all persons, as are the rules of international law. Consequently, it is clear that they who violate these international rules, whether in peace or in war, commit a mortal sin; moreover, in the gravest matters, such as the inviolability of ambassadors, it is not permissible for one country to refuse to be bound by international law, the latter having been established by the authority of the whole world.

For the violation of this law—which is a mortal sin—there exists the court of conscience. There is also, now existing at The Hague—and, appropriately in the Peace Palace—a Permanent Court of International Justice, in which the violations of the law of nations can be determined and righted. We can see the court at The Hague with our own eyes, but the court of conscience is none the less existent, although invisible, and it was to this court to which no less an internationalist than Grotius appealed in behalf of the rights of the Netherlands against the opposition of the Portuguese to Dutch navigation on the high seas and trade without let or hindrance in the islands and territories of the Indian Ocean.

After saying that courts within nations take charge of violations of the law committed within their jurisdictions, and that the Creator of the Universe reserved to Himself punishment of the offenses of nations and their rulers, Grotius adds that there is one tribunal which even the luckiest of sinners does not escape, namely, conscience, or the estimation of one's self, and public opinion, or the estimation of others. "To this double tribunal," he says, "we bring a new case. It is in truth no petty case . . . No! It is a case which concerns practically the entire expanse of the high seas, the right of navigation, the freedom of trade. . . . In this controversy"—between Spain and the Netherlands—"we appeal to those jurists among the Spanish themselves who are especially skilled in both divine and human law; we actually invoke the very laws of Spain itself." [1]

Hitherto, in dealing with the Reading *On the Civil Power* we have been considering the "state" of Victoria, since the state is as a person in this larger state which we call the international community. And just as the inhabitants of a state, such as Spain, his own country, were bound by its national law, so his country, as a "person" of the international community of states, was and is bound hand and foot, as it were, by the law of nations.

Now, "the law of nations," in the Victorian conception, either is natural law or is "derived from natural law," and quoting the *Institutes* of Justinian, Victoria adds: "'What natural reason has established among all nations is called the *jus gentium*.'"

It should be observed that he remarks, in what we would call a sort of offhand way, that a large part at least of this *jus gentium* is synonymous in content with natural law, and that natural law is the source from which it flows. Later on, in the third section of the Reading *On the Indians*, in the opening paragraph of which the definition of international law is given, he completes his idea: "Indeed, there are many things in this connection which

[1] *Mare Liberum*, Carnegie Endowment Edition (New York, 1916), p. 4.

issue from the law of nations, which, because it has a sufficient derivation from natural law, is clearly capable of conferring rights and creating obligations." Here we catch a glimpse in the offing, but nevertheless a glimpse, of the impending sanction.

But to continue Victoria's enlargement of his definition: "even if we grant that it [the law of nations] is not always derived from natural law, yet there exists clearly enough"—What? Nothing more nor less than "a consensus of the greater part of the whole world, especially in behalf of the common good of all." This, in short, defines not only the law but the standard of the law.

Again to continue with Victoria's illustration. "For," he says, "if after the early days of the creation of the world or its recovery from the flood the majority of mankind decided that ambassadors should everywhere be reckoned inviolable and that the sea should be common and that prisoners of war should be made slaves"—at one time they were killed, later enslaved, later still ransomed, and in our day exchanged—"and if this, namely, that strangers should not be driven out, were deemed a desirable principle, it would certainly have the force of law, even though the rest of mankind objected thereto." This is not merely Victoria's law of nations, but the process by which that law of nations may be developed to meet the changing conditions of a changing world.

But Victoria immediately indulges in a further example, which will be peculiarly pleasing to our fellow-countrymen, for in advance he commends their adoption of the rule of *jus soli* in determining nationality: "If children of any Spaniard be born there," he says, meaning in our America, "and they wish to acquire citizenship, it seems they can not be barred either from citizenship or from the advantages enjoyed by other citizens—I refer to the case where the parents had their domicile there." The proof thereof is the law of nations, and one of its rules he now proceeds to apply. "He is to be called and is a citizen who is born within the state." [1] However, the authority is not enough. As a schoolman, he felt the necessity for it to be confirmed, and he says that "the confirmation lies in the fact that, as man is a civil animal, whoever is born in any one state is not a citizen of another state." So reasonable was the enlightened Spaniard that he eliminated by a stroke of his pen, or by a stress of his voice, the stateless person, saying immediately: "Therefore, if he were not a citizen of the state referred to, he would not be a citizen of any state, to the prejudice of his rights under both natural law and the law of nations."

Yet this is not all. The sojourner in the Americas who does not have the good fortune to be born in our part of the world, may become an American by naturalization. "Aye," Victoria continues, "and if there be any persons who wish to acquire a domicile in some state of the Indians, as by marriage or in virtue of any other fact whereby other foreigners are wont to become

[1] Justinian, *Inst.* lib. VIII, tit. 62, §11.

citizens, they can not be impeded any more than others"—here we have the favored nation clause—"and consequently they enjoy the privileges of citizens just as others do"; and the proviso is the law of our day, as well as of his—"provided they also submit to the burdens to which others submit." And though it be against the present immigration law of the United States, which would have excluded many of us were we or our forbears not fortunate enough to have arrived before it was passed, Victoria says expressly that "refusal to receive strangers and foreigners is wrong in itself."

This is a sample of what the Spaniard could say in a couple of paragraphs, and it is therefore no wonder that in two short disquisitions he set forth in essence the law of nations as it was in his day, as it now is, and as it will be in generations, if not centuries, hence.

But what of rights and obligations—or, rather, obligations which are correlative with rights? The matter was one for which Victoria had a predilection, so that he considered it not only in his *Relectio*, but also in his daily lectures to his classes, which, it may be added, are in the course of publication at the present time, several volumes already having appeared containing Victoria's commentaries on the *Secunda Secundae* of St. Thomas.[1]

A certain lecture consisted of a commentary or discussion of Question 40 of the *Secunda Secundae* of St. Thomas on the subject of war; and it is interesting to note—although we may not dwell upon it here—that there are implied, where not expressed, all of Victoria's views on the subject of war, as set forth in his later formal Reading. For our present purpose, however, we can choose but a single passage from the lecture—one which contains not merely the seed but the budding flower of the Victorian conception of sanctions.

"In the case of defensive warfare," Victoria says, "any king whatsoever and any commonwealth whatsoever—for example, this city [meaning the city in which he was lecturing]—may defend themselves"; and the passage which we are quoting is an admirable example of Victoria's method—first in the abstract, then a concrete example: "If the inhabitants of Toledo attack the inhabitants of Salamanca, the latter may defend themselves on their own authority. There can be no doubt on this point. Secondly, I hold," he says, "that the power of the prince is derived from the state. Therefore, in cases in which it is permissible for a state to wage war, it is in like manner permissible for a king to wage war." In our own behalf, we may add, by way of comment, that kings are, as it were, agents of an organized community. "Thirdly," speaking again in the first person, he continues, "I hold that there is a distinction between private persons and states; for, granting that a private person may defend himself and his property, it is nevertheless impermissible for him to avenge himself or to reclaim

---

[1] Edited by R. P. Vicente Beltrán de Heredia, O.P., under the title *Francisco de Vitoria, O.P., Comentarios a la Secunda secundae de Santo Tomás*, and published in the collection *Biblioteca de Teólogos Españoles* issued at Salamanca, Spain. Four volumes of the *Comentarios* have now been published (1932–1934).

his own property save through the judge." Here we have the very heart and soul of Victoria's system. Within the state there is a court of the prince, to which every injured person must resort, unless he is obliged on the instant to defend his life or to maintain his property against the immediate danger of an overwhelming attack. On other occasions the resort must be to law through a court of justice. In a word, Victoria's system is law with a court to interpret the law and to declare the sanction to be applied.

To recur again to Victoria: "For if it were permissible for him to do so in a different manner, that is, if any person whatsoever were the judge of his own cause, it would not be possible to govern the world." Why must this be so? Victoria replies: "For such [a state of affairs] would be contrary not only to divine law, but also to natural law," both of which permit—and indeed require—the organization of a state, under a "prince" or other magistrate, in order to keep peace and tranquillity within the borders of the community. "The state, on the other hand," he goes on to say, "has complete power to avenge itself, to recover its own property, and to punish its enemies," the truth whereof is demonstrated by the fact that, "if the state had not this power, there would be disorder in the world, and injury would be suffered at the hands of the wicked." What, then, is to be done? "Wherefore it follows, that, with respect to these three points—namely, avenging itself upon its enemies, recovering its property, and punishing its enemies—the state possesses the same power over its enemies as that which it possesses over its subjects." And the conclusion? "And if the state has this power, so also has the prince; for he draws his power from the state."

In the association of the artificial persons which we call states of the international community, the international court, in Victoria's day, was lacking, although the process of remedying right and wrong was in its nature and essence judicial.

So much by way of introduction, taken from Victoria's commentary on Question 40 of the *Secunda Secundae* of St. Thomas.

And now a passage from Victoria's Reading *On the Law of War*,[1] in which the sanction makes its material appearance. To begin with, Victoria says: "Princes have authority not only over their own subjects, but also over foreigners, so far as to prevent them from committing wrongs." How can this be so? "By the law of nations and by the authority of the whole world." In the next passage, Victoria adds: "By natural law also, seeing that otherwise society could not hold together unless there was somewhere a power and authority to deter wrongdoers and prevent them from injuring the good and innocent." This power must exist, and because it must exist and is essential to the existence of every organized society, whether group, state or the international community, it is power under the natural law. "Now," declares Victoria, "everything needed for the government and

[1] Quoted from the English translation as published in the Carnegie Institution edition of the *Relectiones* (pp. 163 *et seq.*) above cited.

preservation of society exists by natural law, and in no other way"—he is bold enough to say—"can we show that a State has by natural law authority to inflict pains and penalties on its citizens who are dangerous to it." In this passage, Victoria is speaking, of course, of a single and organized state, for which he has in a sentence provided the sanction, based on natural law, to be used within its borders.   Turning to the international community, he says: "But if a State can do this to its own citizens, society at large"—including in the term "society" that largest of communities which embraces the world at large—"can do it to all wicked and dangerous folk, and this can only be through the instrumentality of princes"—or the agency of the state, as we would say today.   "It is, therefore, certain," he continues, "that princes can punish enemies who have done a wrong to their State and that after a war has been duly and justly undertaken the enemy are just as much within the jurisdiction of the prince who undertakes it as if he were their proper judge."   Here we have the judicial conception of international law applied not merely to the state but to the society of states, requiring for its development and application a court of the prince in the midst of equal states.

"For instance," to use Victoria's own example in a later passage of the same Reading *On War:* "If French brigands made a raid into Spanish territory and the French king would not, though able"—note the word "able"—"compel them to restore their booty, the Spanish might, on the authorization of their sovereign, despoil French merchants or farmers, however innocent these might be."   We are in the presence of a law and the authorization of the sovereign to apply it as against persons who, in judicial terms, would be called the defendant state.   Why does this right of reprisals exist?   "Because," Victoria informs us, "although the French State or Sovereign might initially be blameless, yet it is a breach of duty, as St. Augustine says, for them [the French State or Sovereign] to neglect"—note the word "neglect"—"to vindicate the right against the wrongdoing of their subjects,"—not in their own behalf, but in behalf of the state and of its people,—"and the injured sovereign can take satisfaction from every member and portion of their State."   What is the inner meaning of this, implicit, if not express?   That the defendant king has failed to provide a sanction and a law to carry it into effect, thus manifesting a lamentable lack of that "due diligence" required of both prince and state in international relations.

"An evil and adulterous generation seeketh after a"—sanction; but none other need be given than that of Victoria.

It is universally admitted that there must be relations between nations, for no nation, however large and powerful and possessed of material wealth, is sufficient unto itself.   It is also admitted that there should be a law upon which these relations should be based.   It is generally—although not universally—admitted that the law in such cases is the law of nations; but there

is doubt among the modern "doctors" whether the law international or the law of nations can properly be called law because it lacks a "something", and that "something" is called a "sanction."

Perhaps the simplest way to settle the difference of opinion would be to suggest that there are various kinds of law which culminate in the law of nations. There is what is called "natural law"; there is what is called "divine law"; there is the law of the state, which we call in English, "municipal law"; and there is something indefinable and intangible, and yet vastly important—the law, or, as we generally say, the rule of reason, synonymous, in a sense, with what is called natural law and at the same time a source of law.

As we are dealing with law, it is best to rely upon adjudged cases in which law, recognized as such, has been applied. On the question of sanctions, we cite first *The Prometheus*,[1] decided in the Supreme Court of Hongkong, in 1906, by Sir Henry Spencer Berkeley, Acting Chief Justice, which case was made, as it were, for our present purpose. It was stated that the owners of the *Prometheus*—a Norwegian vessel—took aboard, in the war between Russia and Japan, a cargo to be delivered to a Japanese port. The question involved was whether food-stuffs were, or were not, contraband under the law of nations. In the language of the learned Chief Justice, "it was contended on behalf of the owners of the *Prometheus* that the term 'law,' as applied to this recognized system of principles and rules known as international law, is an inexact expression, that there is, in other words, no such thing as international law; that there can be no such law binding upon all nations, inasmuch as there is no sanction for such law, that is to say, that there is no means by which obedience to such law can be imposed upon any given nation refusing obedience thereto."

What did the Chief Justice, a lawyer to his fingertips and engaged in the administration of the law, say to this? He did not concur: "In my opinion a law may be established and become international, that is to say, binding upon all nations, by the agreement of such nations to be bound thereby, although it may be impossible to enforce obedience thereto by any given nation party to the agreement." Why should this be so? Because "the resistance of a nation to a law to which it has agreed does not derogate from the authority of the law because that resistance can not, perhaps, be overcome." What, then, is the effect? "Such resistance merely makes the resisting nation a breaker of the law to which it has given its adherence, but it leaves the law, to the establishment of which the resisting nation was a party, still subsisting." With this he might have stopped, but he added two further sentences, one a question and the other an answer. The question: "Could it be successfully contended that because any given person or body of persons possessed for the time being power to resist an established municipal law, such law had no existence?" And "the answer to such a contention

[1] 2 Hongkong Law Reports 207 (1906).

would be that the law still existed, though it might not for the time being be possible to enforce obedience to it."

It is to be observed that the learned Chief Justice—and he was indeed learned—was speaking of international law of our day, which he did not define, but it is very material to the present purpose that we have a definition of our day, and what definition could be better than that of Sir Charles Russell, later to be known as Lord Russell of Killowen, a very distinguished practitioner at the bar? He had had experience in international affairs—as had a Chief Justice of the Supreme Court of the United States, who, before his appointment to the Bench, was counsel in the *Alabama case*,[1] and whose authority we shall presently invoke in behalf of municipal sanctions for international law. Sir Charles was counsel for Great Britain in the Bering Sea Arbitration at Paris in 1892, and shortly thereafter he became Lord Chief Justice of Great Britain—the first Catholic raised to that position since the reign of Mary Tudor.

In an address before the American Bar Association in 1896, His Lordship asked the question: "What, then, is international law?"—to which his reply was (and he was not a theorist, but a hard-headed lawyer as well as a distinguished judge upon the Bench): "I know no better definition of it" (meaning international law) "than that it is the sum of the rules or usages which civilized states have agreed shall be binding upon them in their dealings with one another."

The distinguished *prima* professor of theology in the University of Salamanca could not have done better; indeed, it was his view as well as that of the learned Lord Chief Justice, that an "agreement is a pact"; and that a pact is a law which binds both the conscience and the conduct of individuals as well as nations. The difference is a mere question of wording. Writers on law have usually had in mind law as applied to the subjects of a state in their relation to the state and with one another, and that law is generally held to be the command of the superior, that is, of the state, or rather, the sovereign, to the subject—with a material penalty for violation of the law, whether it be fine or imprisonment.

In international relations we are, however, dealing not with a superior and an inferior—as is said to be the case with municipal law (that is, the law of a particular state), but with equals, the theory being that as each state is the equal of the other, there is no superior to prescribe a law to an inferior. Therefore international law—if law be a command of a superior—can not be law. This conclusion, however, does not follow from such a premise; for there may be one kind of law in the case of a state—that of a superior to an inferior—and another kind of law between nations, in which the relationship of superior and inferior does not exist.

Admitting for the sake of argument—although we do not admit it as a

---

[1] The *Alabama* Case, S. Ex. Doc. No. 21, 44th Con., 2d Sess., Report from the Secretary of State, with Accompanying Papers, relating to the Court of Commissioners of Alabama Claims (Washington, 1877) pp. 147, 148.

fact—that law is a command by the sovereign power in a state (as the analytical school of English jurisprudence insists), it must nevertheless be pointed out that there is a kind of law even within states which is not a command; for indeed, the common law of England was not a command from the sovereign, although its violation is subject to a penalty.   If that be so, it follows that a command is not a necessary element either to a law or to its sanction.   It is therefore very material to inquire, then, what is common law?   It is frequent usage developing into a custom which, accepted as law, is applied as law through and by courts of justice.   The analytical school, however, goes on the theory that what the king permits he commands; hence, the common law, being permitted by the king, is commanded by the king and therefore enforced through the king's courts of justice.   Permission, it is to be said, is, however, not a command but is in fact a recognition and acceptance of the custom.   Therefore, in the manner of the schoolmen, we may take it as proved that the common law, at least, is not a command.

If there can be law within a state without command, may there not be a law between states without a command?   May we not say that in the latter, as in the case of the common law, command is absent, since between and among equals there can be no superior?

Now as there is a common law of the state, so there may be a common law of the states or nations, but between the states there can not be, even upon the basis of the arguments of the analytical school, a common law which is a command, because among equals there can be no superior whose permission can be distorted into a command.   How does this common law of nations arise?   Frequent usage of nations becomes hardened into the custom of nations, and through the adoption by nations of these universal customs, they become the common law of nations by the tacit agreement of the nations, evidenced by their application of customs in their mutual relations.

Just as the common law in England assumed definite form and shape through the decisions of courts, so the common law of nations has, in the course of centuries, assumed definite form and shape through the practice of nations.   The process, differing in form, is essentially the same in each case; therefore the result should be and is the same.   The only difference is that courts of justice exist within the state to apply the customary law in question in suits brought in such courts, the cases being thus decided by judges learned in the law; while on the other hand there has been until recently no court between the nations, although from antiquity to the present day, there have been temporary mixed commissions or tribunals of arbitration created by *agreement* of the parties—that is to say, the states—to decide disputes which have arisen between them and which it has been the desire of the states to settle without a resort to war.   In these tribunals, as well as in the Permanent Court of International Justice at the Hague, we have a court without a superior, created by the *agreement* of nations, with a law which it administers,

whether it be custom, "as evidence of a general practice accepted as law," [1] or agreements in the form of pacts, "having the force of law," according to Victoria's statement.

The definition of law as the command of a sovereign—a command which does not exist in customary law, forming a large part of the law of England—can not be said to be essential to the existence of law; and the common law of nations, consisting of generally recognized customs, is even less the command of superiors than are the customs of England. Pacts of equal states—for what state ever voluntarily recognizes itself as inferior to another—are agreements. According to Victoria, pacts are laws and bind those who have entered into them voluntarily. In short, not only customs but pacts, are voluntary, without the necessary intervention of a sovereign within the state or between the states except as agent of the respective peoples.

But there is another kind of law—positive law, as it is called. This is the law of a king or other ruler, possessed of the right to make law, or of a legislature, having the power to enact laws. Therefore it is said to be the law of the sovereign. Assuredly, however, it is not the law of a personal sovereign, for such a sovereign no longer makes law in civilized states or communities. He is, for instance, a party to the law-making power in Great Britain, with the right to veto an act of Parliament, which right to veto has not been exercised these many years. In the United States, the Congress, composed of a Senate and a House of Representatives, enacts a law, which, to become effective, requires the approval of the President of the United States; or, to be passed over his veto, it requires the vote of two-thirds of both houses. It is only as a legal fiction, therefore, that the acts of the British Parliament and the acts of the American Congress can be said to be positive law in the sense of a command. But to speak only of the United States, we know that the source of power in each of the American states is vested in the people—men and women—of the states. We know that the legislators who pass acts do so as representatives of the people and that the legislator is their agent, not their master.

Thus it is that the members of the Senate—ninety-six in number—are elected by the men and women of the different states of the American Union, and the members of the House are elected by the states in proportion to their respective populations and within what are called Congressional districts of the individual states. The senators are therefore the representatives of the peoples of the individual states, and the members of the House of Representatives—there is an argument in the very name—are the authorized agents of the voters within their districts—men and women, without distinction of sex, exercising the right to vote. How can it be said that an act of Congress is a command, unless it be a command of the people—from below, not above? The theory of positive law as a command is not only monarchical but it is also archaic. Law in this modern world of ours is not a command;

[1] Statute of the Permanent Court of International Justice at The Hague, Article 38 (2).

it is the authority and consent of the people given in advance to the enactment of laws which, in the opinion of their chosen agents are necessary for the common good within the state. Whether the laws be national or local, the process is the same, for the legislatures of each state are composed of a lower and an upper house corresponding to the Senate and the House of Representatives of the United States, with the right on the part of the Governor to veto, which veto can be overridden by the two houses of each of the states.

Suppose, however, the act within the state is passed by the legislature and approved by the Governor, but is displeasing to the people of the state. The act will be repealed, because the agency is subject to the principal.

In the same way, the Congress is but the agency of the people of the different states, and an act of Congress which is obnoxious to the people in their united capacity will be repealed. Indeed, the most solemn of laws—an amendment to the Constitution of the United States—which meets with the disapproval of the people of the states is subject to repeal; and within the past year the eighteenth amendment to the Constitution of the United States, forbidding the manufacture and sale of intoxicating liquors, was repealed on the 5th day of December, 1933. The repeal of an amendment requires the concurrence of three-fourths of the states, either by their respective legislatures or by conventions especially called and elected for this purpose, as in the case at hand. This is indeed the consent of the governed; this is the Declaration of Independence in action—of government by the consent of the governed.

If this be the doctrine within every republic of the Western World—of which there are twenty-one—we are justified in believing that it either is or will be the doctrine with every other modern state, so that even if we argue by analogy, there is no need for us to change or attempt to change the conception of international law as a thing of custom or pact, because the theory of the state where once a sovereign power above and beyond the people was exercised by a personal sovereign, has given way to government "of the people, by the people and for the people." Government by command involves a power superior to that of those who are commanded. Government by consent is the only form of government consistent with the nature and dignity of human beings.

Victoria does not express himself on this aspect of law in such definite terms; but what is his government by majorities except government by consent? And therefore within his state, as between nations, there is consent—which is not a command—and between states there are agreements, which negative a command. Therefore we need not trouble ourselves about the definitions of theorists of our day or of writers of the past, who insist that law is a command of a sovereign power above the people forming the state.

Let us consider the statement of Victoria in reference to the international community—"the world as a whole, being in a way one single State." He

has proved, as we have seen, that laws are made in the state and that they bind both the legislature and the king even though the act of creating the law be voluntary on the part of the king—and I add, the chief executive, to bring his statement up to date; and that it does not depend upon the will of the legislature or the chief executive that one or the other is bound. Also in the case of pacts, one who enters into a pact of his own free will is nevertheless bound thereby. The pact is an agreement, and a first principle of natural law is that pacts, although entered into voluntarily—and they should be so entered into—are to be kept. *Pacta sunt servanda.*

Proceeding from the group forming the state to the group of states forming the international community, Victoria infers a corollary: "that international law has not only the force of a pact and agreement among men, but also the force of a law." The reason is that "the world as a whole, being in a way one single State, has the power to create laws that are just and fitting for all persons"—that is to say, for all persons of each and every group of individuals and of all states forming the international community—"as are the rules of international law." Here we have the groups of individuals associated for a political and social and moral purpose to form a state, and the states in turn forming the international community; and as the state represents the individuals and the group within state lines, so the international community represents the individuals and the states composing the international community.

It is easy enough for us to see all this today. It was not an easy thing for Victoria in his day and generation. Yet he divined the international community, although he did not create it. Indeed, he not only recognized the existence of, but defined, the community which existed of itself, irrespective of the will or the action of any man or of any group; for the international community existed *ex jure necessitatis.*

Now let us suppose that a person residing within a state violates the law of the state. According to Victoria, if the case be one of sufficient gravity, he commits a mortal sin, cognizable in the court of conscience. It is also cognizable in a court of justice; for the law of the state has a double sanction —the one spiritual, in the court of conscience, and the other material, in a court of justice. The great Grotius recognized this and stated it in unmistakable and incontrovertible terms in his address to the Christian Princes, prefixed to his tractate on the *Freedom of the Seas.* What, then, of international rules, the law of each and every state? "Consequently," Victoria says, "it is clear that they who violate these international rules, whether in peace or in war, commit a mortal sin"; and he adds that "in the gravest matters, such as the inviolability of ambassadors, it is not permissible for one country to refuse to be bound by international law." Why? "The latter having been established by the authority of the whole world."

Let us analyze this sentence—for it is but a sentence. We have international rules. But whether they be customs or agreements, or whether the

violations of them be in peace or in war, in the cases which we have in mind, there is no command involved. These rules have arisen from customs; or they are express agreements as in the case of pacts. Now, in the Victorian conception, these customary rules, although they are not agreements, in the sense of pacts, are binding, as are pacts, because Victoria selects as his example the inviolability of ambassadors, which inviolability arose from the custom and the practice of nations, and not by municipal statute or by pact; and the custom being general, no country can refuse to be bound by the rule concerning the inviolability of ambassadors—and therefore, through its agent, the state, being bound by international law, commits a mortal sin if it violates the immunity of ambassadors, a sin cognizable alike in the court of conscience and in a court of justice.

What is the implication of all this? If, by the constitutional law of a state, an act of the legislative body be required in order to carry out the rule of international law, then it is the duty of the nation in question to pass such a municipal statute, and if it does not pass the municipal act, it is liable for damages to the nation or to the individual who may have suffered by its failure so to do. As Victoria frequently chooses the immunity of ambassadors in order to make his meaning clear—inasmuch as the immunities of diplomatic agents are universal and may therefore be considered as "established by the authority of the whole world"—let us test the appositeness of the illustration by a few decisions of municipal courts dealing with such immunities.

The first case is one of more than passing interest.[1] It happened in the lifetime of Peter the Great, Czar of all the Russias, whose empire had formally made its entry into the international community. One Andrew Artemonowitz Matueof had been appointed "ambassador extraordinary of his czarish majesty, emperor of Great Russia, her majesty's [Queen Anne's] good friend and ally". It appeared that his excellency was arrested and taken "by violence, out of his coach in the public street," and "he was detained in custody for several hours, in contempt of the protection granted by her majesty, contrary to the law of nations and in prejudice of the rights and privileges which ambassadors and other public ministers, authorized and received as such, have at all times been thereby possessed of, and ought to be kept sacred and inviolable".

As a result of this incident there was an act of Parliament passed in the year 1708, to carry into effect the law of nations relating to the immunity of ambassadors and public ministers, an immunity under the law of nations which had been recognized time out of mind. When the case of the Ambassador of Muscovy—for so he was called in the suit—was tried in the eighth year of the reign of Queen Anne, that is, in 1710, in the Queen's Bench, before Lord Chief Justice Holt, the question before the court was whether an

---

[1] The Case of Andrew Artemonowitz Matueof, Ambassador of Muscovy, 10 Mod. 5 (1710).

ambassador could lawfully be arrested for debt—or for any other cause. The case was argued by the Attorney-General, Sir James Montague (later Chief Baron of the Exchequer), in behalf of the ambassador, and the Attorney-General said roundly that the ambassador could not be arrested, and then proceeded to state the reasons, as applicable then as they are today: "If the privileges of an ambassador may by law be broken in upon and invaded for the preservation of the property of a private subject, princes will be cautious of sending ambassadors to us; ours must expect the like treatment." This we consider to be a question of general right—not merely immunity from suit for indebtedness. After stating that "few will be prevailed with to take that character [of ambassador] upon them," the Attorney-General continued, "should an ambassador be liable to the restraints of the law of the land to which he goes, how easy would it be, upon an emergency, to take off his attendance upon his master's business?" Here we have two reasons: that ambassadors would be unwilling to subject themselves to arrest or restraint; and that, under such circumstances, not merely the ambassador, but the business of his master, would or might suffer. The practice of nations was clearly in favor of immunity; for "the person of an ambassador," the Attorney-General continued, "has ever been held sacred and inviolable by the law of nations". Neither his property nor his person is liable to arrest. There should, however, be a remedy available to prevent abuse of the inviolability; otherwise unscrupulous ambassadors, or other diplomatic agents, might avail themselves of their immunity to violate the laws of the country to which they were accredited. What, then, is the way of preventing this? "An ambassador must be intreated," the Attorney-General further continued, "and upon refusal sent back to his master," the theory being that the country which he represents still exercises exclusive jurisdiction over his person and property, so that, in case he commits an offense or a crime within the country to which he is accredited, he should be returned to the jurisdiction of the country whereof he is the diplomatic agent.

The Attorney-General next dwells upon the representative character of the ambassador, asserting that nobody would say that "the Czar himself might have been arrested," and that "the same fiction of law that makes him [the ambassador] represent the person of his master, makes him extra-parochial, and quasi, in the dominions of his master." And, finally, that "the ill treatment of ambassadors is a thing of dangerous consequence, for it may involve the nation in a war, and it would be very inconvenient that this should be in the power of any private person whatsoever."

The persons implicated were arrested, examined before the privy council, and seventeen were committed to prison. They were tried and convicted on the facts by the jury, but no sentence was rendered.

The case of *Triquet* v. *Bath* [1] involved also the question of diplomatic

[1] 3 Burr. 1478 (1764).

immunities.   It was tried in 1764, in the Court of King's Bench, before Lord Chief Justice Mansfield, who decided that "the privilege of foreign ministers and their domestic servants depends upon the law of nations," and that, to quote his exact words, "all that is new in this act [1] is the clause which gives a summary jurisdiction for the punishment of the infractors of this law."

His Lordship then proceeded to recount in an interesting and indeed, entertaining way, for his judgments were literature as well as law, the facts in the case of the Ambassador from Muscovy—the wrath of the Czar and the humiliation of Great Britain, resulting in a special embassy and an illumi- nated apology to his "czarish majesty."   His exact language we quote, lest inadvertently we do an injustice to my Lord Mansfield or to the Czar:

. . . The act of Parliament was made upon occasion of the Czar's ambassador being arrested.   If proper application had been immediately made for his discharge from the arrest, the matter might and doubtless would have been set right.   Instead of that, bail was put in, before any complaint was made.   An information was filed by the then Attorney- General against the persons who were thus concerned, as infractors of the law of nations, and they were found guilty, but never brought up to judgment.

The Czar took the matter up, highly.   No punishment would have been thought, by him, an adequate reparation.   Such a sentence as the court could have given, he might have thought a fresh insult.

Another expedient was fallen upon and agreed to; this Act of Parliament passed, as an apology and humiliation from the whole nation.   It was sent to the Czar, finely illuminated, by an ambassador extraordinary, who made excuses in a solemn oration.

A great deal relative to this transaction and negotiation appears in the annals of that time; and from a correspondence of the Secretary of State there printed.

But the Act was not occasioned by any doubt 'whether the law of nations, particularly the part relative to public ministers, was not part of the law of England, and the infraction, criminal; nor intended to vary an iota from it'.

In an earlier case on the subject—that of *Buvot* v. *Barbut*,[2] decided in 1736 by Lord Chancellor Talbot—Lord Mansfield, then known as William Mur- ray and practising at the London bar, appeared as counsel in the case.   As Lord Mansfield said, in the course of his opinion in the case of *Triquet* v. *Bath*, that he "was counsel in this case," and had "a full note of it", prefer- ence should naturally be given to his statement of the matter.   "These questions arose," he said, "and were discussed.   'Whether a minister could, by any act or acts, waive his privilege.'   'Whether being a trader was any objection against allowing privilege to a minister, personally.'   'Whether an agent of commerce, or even a consul, was entitled to the privileges of a public minister.'   'What was the rule of decision: the act of Parliament or the law of nations.'"   His lordship continued: "Lord Talbot declared a clear opinion—'That the law of nations, in its full extent, was part of the law of England.'   'That the act of Parliament was declaratory, and occasioned by a particular incident.'   'That the law of nations was to be collected from the practice of different nations, and the authority of writers.'   Accordingly, he argued and determined from such instances, and the authority of Grotius,

[1] 7 Anne, c. 12 (1708).   [2] Cas. *temp.* Talbot 281, 25 E. R. 777 (1736).

Barbeyrac, Binkershoek, Wiquefort, &c.; there being no English writer of eminence upon the subject."

Three years after the case of *Triquet* v. *Bath*, Lord Mansfield considered a like question in *Heathfield* v. *Chilton*,[1] in part confirming what he had said in the previous case, making, however, a very precious addition: "The privileges of public ministers and their retinue depend upon the law of nations;[2] which is part of the common law of England. And the act of Parliament of 7 Anne, c. 12, did not intend to alter, nor can alter the law of nations."

What conclusions are to be drawn from these three leading cases, each dealing with the nature and extent of diplomatic immunity? In the first place, it is to be observed that the immunity was that of the law of nations—a law existing previous to the statute of Queen Anne. In the second place, it is to be further observed, that the law of nations was the law of England—not statute law, but common law, resulting from the practice of nations. In the third place, that it was a law superior to any other law in England, in that it could not be modified by an act of Parliament. And finally, that the statute was expressly passed to provide the rule of the law of nations with a municipal sanction, and that, in so doing, it recognized the law of nations as an existing and obligatory law. The right to immunity, and the duty of England to protect that right, existed. The duty was not created by the statute; it existed under international law, and, because the statute had not theretofore existed, Great Britain passed it, in order that the violation of the immunity of diplomatic agents under international law should not happen again.

It is to be observed that the three cases are English cases. But, as the common law of England became the law of the Colonies and was continued without modification when they became States, in so far as international law is concerned, the English cases were American precedents. An early and a leading and an interesting case is that of *Nathan* v. *Commonwealth of Virginia*,[3] tried in the Court of Common Pleas of Philadelphia County, in the State of Pennsylvania, in the September Term of 1781, when our Washington, to whom reference is made, was paying his respects to Cornwallis, temporarily residing at Yorktown. It appears that a quantity of clothing belonging to the commonwealth of Virginia was imported from France, and one Simon Nathan, claiming an interest in the property, caused a foreign attachment to be issued against Virginia, and the clothing was attached in Philadelphia. "The delegates in Congress from Virginia,"—then sitting in Pennsylvania—"conceiving this a violation of the laws of nations, applied

---

[1] 4 Burr. 2015 (1767).

[2] The law of nations which Lord Mansfield had in mind was stated in the report of the Law Officers of the Crown in the famous diplomatic case of the Silesian loan to which his Lordship, as William Murray, then Solicitor-General, affixed his name—if the definition did not actually come from his hand: "The Law of Nations is founded upon Justice, Equity, Convenience, and the Reason of the Thing, and confirmed by long Usage, . . .—Rt. Hon. Sir Ernest Satow, *The Silesian Loan and Frederick the Great* (Oxford, 1915), p. 82.

[3] 1 Dall. 77 n. (1781).

to the Supreme Executive Council of Pennsylvania, by whom the sheriff was ordered to give up the goods."

The case was elaborately argued by the Attorney-General of the Commonwealth of Pennsylvania and by counsel for the plaintiff. The court decided that the property of a sister state was not liable to attachment in Philadelphia. As the judgment was rendered without an opinion and in accordance with the views of the Attorney-General, only the material portion of his argument dealing with the principle in question will be considered. "He premised, that though the several states which form our federal republic, had, by the confederation,"—which had gone into effect on the 1st of March, 1781—"ceded many of the prerogatives of sovereignty to the United States, yet these voluntary engagements did not injure their independence on each other; but that each was a sovereign, 'with every power, jurisdiction and right, not expressly given up.'" His argument consisted of two points: "First: that every kind of process, issued against a sovereign, is a violation of the laws of nations; and is in itself null and void. Second: that a sheriff cannot be compelled to serve or return a void writ."

The first point the Attorney-General "endeavoured to prove, by considering, first, the nature of sovereignty; and, secondly, the rules of law, relative to process issued against ambassadors, the representatives of sovereigns," relying upon Vattel, who was before, and apparently still is after, their independence, the principal authority on international law in the United States—and in the Supreme Court since its organization.

Having stated that there was no instance in our law books of a process against a sovereign, the Attorney-General considered suits against their representatives. The stock example, of course, was the immunity of diplomatic officers, existing by the law of nations, the violation of which was to be punished [in England] under the famous statute of 7 Queen Anne, c. 12, which statute, he said, did not introduce the immunity of diplomatic agents, but was merely "declaratory of the law of nations," with "nothing new in it, except the clause prescribing a summary mode of punishment"; and he concluded, under this heading, that this statute was a "part of the common law of the land before, and consequently extended to Pennsylvania." His authorities were Blackstone's *Commentaries*,[1] and the cases of *Triquet* v. *Bath* and *Heathfield* v. *Chilton*.

Since the writ of the sheriff was null and void against a representative, as against the sovereign, it followed that the sheriff attaching the goods in question was liable to punishment, and to show the "inconveniences" which would follow, the Attorney-General referred to the calamity which might happen to the body politic, if the sheriff could lawfully attach the goods addressed to a sovereign or its representative: "that any disaffected person, who happened to be a creditor of the United States, might injure our public defence, and retard or ruin the operations of a campaign; that he

[1] 4 Bl. Comm. 67.

might issue an attachment against the cannon of General Washington, or seize the public money designed for the payment of his army."

The allusion to Washington was not accidental.   As appears by his diary, his army, marching toward Yorktown, arrived in Philadelphia on the 31st of August, and on the 5th of September there is an entry concerning "the rear of the French Army having reached Philadelphia and the American's having passed it." [1]

There is a later case in Pennsylvania which is even more interesting.   It is that of *Republica* v. *de Longchamps* [2] in the Court of Oyer and Terminer at Philadelphia in 1784.   The facts were that the Chevalier de Longchamps, an officer of the French Army in America, was indicted on the charge that he "unlawfully and insolently did threaten and menace bodily harm and violence to the person of . . . François Barbé-Marbois" in the residence of the French Minister Plenipotentiary.   M. Barbé-Marbois was then Secretary of the French Legation and Consul General of France to the United States.   It was specifically stated in the indictment that M. Barbé-Marbois was at the time "under the protection of the law of nations, and this commonwealth"; and that, on the 19th of May, the Chevalier de Longchamps, in the public street, "unlawfully, premeditatedly and violently" assaulted M. Barbé-Marbois, striking him "in violation of the laws of nations, against the peace and dignity of the United States and of the Commonwealth of Pennsylvania."

The Attorney-General, assisted by none other than the famous James Wilson, a signer of the Declaration of Independence, soon to be a member from Pennsylvania of the Federal Convention in Philadelphia, to the success of which he largely contributed, and still later to be an original member of the Supreme Court appointed by President Washington, appeared for the prosecution.   They advocated "the necessity of sustaining the law of nations, of protecting and securing the persons and privileges of ambassadors;" —to quote the exact language of the report—"the connection between the law of nations and the municipal law, and the effect which the decision of this case must have upon the honor of Pennsylvania, and the safety of her citizens abroad".

In support of their contention, they invoked the authority of Blackstone's *Commentaries*, [3] *Triquet* v. *Bath*, [4] and Vattel's *Law of Nature and of Na-*

---

[1] *The Diaries of George Washington* (1748–1799), ed. by John Fitzpatrick (Boston and New York, 1925), Vol. ii, p. 258.   [2] 1 Dall. 111 (1784).

[3] 1 Bl. Comm. 253.

[4] In this case, Lord Mansfield, after saying, "I was counsel in this case"—meaning that of Buvot *v.* Barbut, before Lord Talbot—"and have a full note of it," continues without a break: "I remember, too, Lord Hardwicke's declaring his opinion to the same effect; and denying that Lord Chief Justice Holt ever had any doubt as to the law of nations being part of the law of England, upon the occasion of the arrest of the Russian ambassador."

Chief Justice McKean refers in the decision of *Respublica* v. *De Longchamps*, to "the case of the Russian ambassador": "A wrong opinion has been entertained concerning the conduct of Lord Chief Justice Holt and the court of king's bench, in England, in the noted case of the Russian ambassador.   They detained the offenders, after conviction, in prison, from

tions.[1] If M. Barbé-Marbois, they added, had "been prevented from paying a proper attention to his appointments", this would have been "certainly a violation of the law of nations," citing in this respect Vattel.[2] "Upon the same principle"—to quote from the argument as reported—"that the infringement of a statute is an indictable offence, though the mode of punishment is not pointed out in the act itself, an offence against the laws of nations, while they compose a part of the law of the land, must necessarily be indictable".

Chief Justice McKean, a man of large political and judicial experience and himself a signer of the Declaration of Independence, stated the trial to be a case of "first impression in the United States"; that it was to be determined "on the principles of the laws of nations, which form a part of the municipal law of Pennsylvania".

The jury returned a verdict of "guilty", first on the assault count and later on both counts.

The case being considered of "first impression in the United States", the sentence of the court of first instance was suspended and the case stayed for the opinion of the judges.   It was very carefully argued, as appears from the report and from the opinion rendered by Mr. Chief Justice McKean, in the course of which, after stating that the crime was an infraction of the law of nations, he added that "this law, in its full extent, is a part of the law of this state, and is to be collected from the practice of different nations, and the authority of writers"; that "the person of a public minister is sacred and inviolable"; and that "whoever offers any violence to him, not only affronts

---

term to term, until the Czar Peter was satisfied, without ever proceeding to judgment; and from this, it has been inferred, that the court doubted, whether they could inflict any punishment for an infraction of the law of nations.   But this was not the reason.   The court never doubted, that the law of nations formed a part of the law of England, and that a violation of this general law could be punished by them; but no punishment less than death would have been thought by the Czar an adequate reparation for the arrest of his ambassador.   This punishment they could not inflict, and such a sentence as they could have given, he might have thought a fresh insult.   Another expedient was, therefore, fallen upon. However, the princes of the world, at this day, are more enlightened, and do not require impracticable nor unreasonable reparations for injuries of this kind."

The above passage from Chief Justice McKean's opinion pronouncing judgment is here reproduced, in order to show the care with which the case of *Respublica* v. *De Longchamps* was considered and the judicial precedents examined and mastered regarding the law of nations as the law universal and therefore the law of each and every state.

There is an incident mentioned in *Appleton's Encyclopaedia of American Biography* (1st ed. 1888), vol. iv, p. 199, in the article on "François de Barbé-Marbois," which shows that time left undimmed the Marquis de Barbé-Marbois' interest in things American:

"Just before Lafayette's death Marbois invited him, with the American minister and several of the latter's compatriots, including Col. Nicolas Fish, to dine with him.   Before the repast the company was shown into a room that was in strong contrast with the other elegant apartments.   It looked like a large room in a Dutch or Belgian farmhouse.   On a long, rough table was spread a dinner in keeping with the room: a single dish of meat, uncouth pastry, and wine in bottles and decanters, accompanied by glasses and silver goblets. 'Do you know where we are?' said Marbois to Lafayette and the other guests.   The marquis looked at the low ceiling with its heavy, bare beams, and, after a brief pause, exclaimed: 'Ah! the seven doors, and the one window, and the silver goblets, such as the marshal of France used in my youth!   My friends, we are in Washington's headquarters, on the Hudson fifty years ago.'"

[1] Vattel, *Law of Nations* (1760), pref. 6, p. 203; lib. 1, § 6; lib. 4, §§ 80, 84.
[2] *Ibid.*, lib. 2, § 218.

the sovereign he represents, but also hurts the common safety and well-being of nations"; and such being the case, that "he is guilty of a crime against the whole world".

The *Longchamps* case was not a whit less interesting than *Triquet* v. *Bath*, and it makes an even stronger appeal to us of America, not merely because of its historical associations, but because of the argument of counsel and the opinion of the Chief Justice.

In passing, it may be said that it is also the first case, so far as is known, of a request for extradition from the United States on the part of a foreign government—in this instance, France, and de Longchamps the person to be extradited—which the court, after grave deliberation, refused on the ground that the offense was committed in the United States and should be tried where committed. In the argument, as we have seen, it was maintained that the law of nations being a part of the law of the land, the offense was as indictable as if under a statute, in that the law of nations, being the law of the land, had the effect of a statute, and that a person violating the law of nations was guilty of a crime against the whole world, and that not merely the law of the state in which the offense was committed was violated, but the right of every state of the civilized world was violated by the violation of international law, wherever it took place.

We are indeed deeply indebted to the argument of James Wilson and to the opinion of Thomas W. McKean, Chief Justice of Pennsylvania.

But important as the case is, and interesting as it must be admitted to be, it is perhaps more interesting by virtue of the persons involved; more so, perhaps, than any other case decided in our courts. François, Marquis de Barbé-Marbois was not merely Consul General and Secretary of the Legation, who, as such, performed his duties to the satisfaction of his government during the period of our Revolution, but later he it was who advised M. de Vergennes, then Minister of Foreign Affairs of France, not to recommend a foreigner as the first Bishop of the Catholic Church in the United States and (if he recommended anybody) to name one John Carroll, who would be most acceptable because highly thought of in the United States.[1] In addition, it was through the same Marquis de Barbé-Marbois, Minister of State of the great Napoleon, that the proposition was made to Robert R. Livingston, then our Minister to France, to cede the vast territory of Louisiana to the United States.

If we now turn to the Constitution of the United States,[2] we find that

[1] See the article by the Rev. Jules A. Baisnée entitled, *The Myth of the " French Scheme for the Enslavement of American Catholics"* (1783–1784), published in the Catholic Historical Review, Vol. xix, No. 4, January, 1934, pp. 437–459; also his *France and the Establishment of the American Catholic Hierarchy: the Myth of French Interference, 1783–1784* (Baltimore, 1934).
[2] The text from this point to the discussion of the Arjona case (*infra*, p. 43), is reproduced by permission, with an occasional modification, from a presidential address entitled "International Law, Municipal Law, and Their Sanctions," delivered before the American Society of International Law on April 27, 1933, and printed in the *Proceedings* of the Society for 1933, pp. 5–33.

Congress has the power "to define and punish," let us say, without quoting, offenses against international law, specifying some and including all others by the words, "offenses against the law of nations."[1] The word "piracy" is used. But what if it is not defined? Then, of course, it is piracy under the law of nations. If, however, it is defined by Congress, it is still according to the law of nations, for if the definition of the United States differs from the meaning under the law of nations, the statute is an attempt to set up a definition inconsistent with the law of nations and is, to the extent of the inconsistency, null and void as against the nations. Why is this so? Because a statute of the United States, even if dealing with the law of nations, is an unilateral act and therefore can only bind the United States and be exercised within their jurisdiction.

The best case, perhaps, on the subject is *United States* v. *Smith*,[2] decided in 1820. The defendant Smith was indicted for piracy under an act of Congress of March 3, 1819,[3] providing "that if any person or persons whatsoever, shall, on the high seas, commit the crime of piracy, as defined by the law of nations, and such offender or offenders shall afterwards be brought into, or found in, the United States, every such offender or offenders shall, upon conviction thereof, before the circuit court of the United States for the district into which he or they may be brought, or in which he or they shall be found, be punished with death." Here we have the exact case of the Constitution, by virtue of which Congress is authorized "to define and punish . . . Piracies," etc. So much for the first question raised.

The second was whether the crime of piracy was defined by the law of nations with reasonable accuracy. The opinion in the case was that of the learned Justice Story, who said in this connection: "What the law of nations on this subject is, may be ascertained by consulting the works of jurists, writing professedly on public laws; or by the general usage and practice of nations; or by judicial decisions recognizing and enforcing that law." What, then, was the definition under the law of nations? "Robbery, or forcible depredations upon the sea, *animo furandi*, is piracy." Then, too, he says, great writers on maritime law profess the same doctrine, and the common law to which he refers "recognises and punishes piracy as an offence, not against its own municipal code, but as an offence against the law of nations (which is part of the common law)"—it is Justice Story who is speaking—"as an offence against the universal law of society, a pirate being deemed an enemy of the human race."[4] Here we have the law of nations considered

---

[1] Art. viii, § 10. [2] 5 Wheat. 153 (1820).

[3] An Act to protect the commerce of the United States and punish the crime of piracy. 3 Stat. 513 (1819), 33 U. S. Code, § 383 (1926).

[4] For a more elaborate statement of Justice Story's conception of the law of nations and its sources, see *La Jeune Eugénie*, 2 Mason 409, Fed. Cas. No. 15,551 (1822). Arranged in seven numbered parts, the statement reads:

"(1) Now the law of nations may be deduced, first, from the general principles of right and justice, applied to the concerns of individuals, and thence to the relations and duties of nations; or (2) secondly, in things indifferent or questionable, from the customary observances and recognitions of civilized nations; or, (3) lastly, from the conventional or positive

as an integral part of the law of the United States, and the offense or the felony is sufficiently defined, "whether we advert to writers on the common law, or the maritime law, or the law of nations"; that is to say, the law of nations binding upon every nation is a part of the municipal law of every nation, to be rendered effective in case of need by a municipal statute, the offense being under international law and the punishment under a municipal statute. A case of piracy, however, is of a very general nature. Although a pirate's acts may bring him under the definition of piracy under the law of nations, he is regarded as not acting under the law of any country and is to be tried for the offense in any country within whose jurisdiction he may be brought.

There are many interesting cases of an international nature punishable by a municipal sanction. Speaking within the jurisdiction of the United States, it will suffice for us to cite a few American cases dealing with neutrality. The law of neutrality used to confer an equal right upon both belligerents. Thus in the time of Grotius it was stated by that great man to be within the right of neutral nations to allow a belligerent to cross its territory on condition that the same right were accorded to the other belligerent. But Grotius also allowed the neutral to grant preferred treatment to the belligerent whose cause was just as against the belligerent with an unjust cause. This latter conception of neutrality, however, has been disregarded, as it involves the exercise, on the part of the neutral, of the function of a judge, deciding the cause of the war, one or the other of the belligerents to be adjudged right or wrong, according to the view of the neutral. This was not the American conception, which was that the neutral should be "neuter" in the sense that he should take no part in the contest and that, if an American citizen did so, it was at his peril; and a statute of the United States to that effect was passed in 1794,[1] the first municipal statute upon this international right or duty. President Washington's administration was of the opinion that the offense was under international law and that, as international law was the law of the land, it did not require a statute. However, to remove any possible doubt on the question, and to provide definite penalties, the statute was passed making the violation of neutrality a municipal offense

---

law, that regulates the intercourse between states. (4) What, therefore, the law of the nations is, does not rest upon mere theory, but may be considered, as modified by practice, or ascertained by the treaties of nations at different periods. (5) It does not follow, therefore, that because a principle cannot be found settled by the consent or practice of nations at one time, it is to be concluded, that at no subsequent period the principle can be considered as incorporated into the public code of nations. (6) Nor is to be admitted, that no principle belongs to the law of nations, which is not universally recognized, as such, by all civilized communities, or even by those constituting, what may be called, the Christian states of Europe. . . . (7) But I think it may be unequivocally affirmed, that every doctrine that may be fairly deduced by correct reasoning from the rights and duties of nations, and the nature of moral obligation, may theoretically be said to exist in the law of nations; and unless it be relaxed or waived by the consent of nations, which may be evidenced by their general practice and customs, it may be enforced by a court of justice, whenever it arises in judgment. . . ."

[1] Neutrality Act of 1794, 1 Stat. 381 (1794).

and creating a municipal punishment for the violation of international law thus specifically recognized by the statute of the United States. The neutrality statute in question warned American citizens against trading in contraband and blockade, in that they might be captured by the belligerent whose cause was injured by such trade, even though the offense were committed on the high seas outside of the jurisdiction of any nation.

Let us consider two situations, with which we are familiar,—perhaps too familiar, as they are taken from the so-called law of war—for I have often wondered how an illegal thing can claim to be a thing of law. The first deals with the law of neutrality, and the second, with an offense upon the high seas, without reference to neutrality.

Let us suppose that a belligerent vessel is lying within the territorial waters of the United States and that an individual, native or foreign, enlists himself as a member of the foreign crew. This is a violation of a statute of the United States designed to carry into effect what President Washington's government believed to be the neutral duty of the United States, and therefore of its citizens. It was not a law passed at random; it was passed because of the fear in many quarters that the rule of international law did not carry with it a municipal penalty. Therefore the Neutrality Act of June 5, 1794, was passed for the express purpose of making a municipal duty by statute what President Washington and his advisers considered an international duty without statute. Here we have a municipal sanction of an admitted principle of the law of nations.

Let us take as an illustration an early case in the history of the United States. It is that of Gideon Henfield,[1] who in 1793 was charged with having illegally enlisted on a French privateer, the *Citizen Genet*, at Charleston, South Carolina, and with having taken part in the capture of a British vessel at a time when the United States was at peace with Great Britain. The trial took place before the Circuit Court of the United States for the Pennsylvania District, and the case was argued before Judges Wilson, Iredell and Peters. The former, in his charge to the jury, said:

It is the joint and unanimous opinion of the Court, that the United States, being in a state of neutrality relative to the present war, the acts of hostility committed by Gideon Henfield are an offence against this country, and punishable by its laws.

It has been asked by his counsel, in their address to you, against what law has he offended? The answer is, against many and binding laws. As a citizen of the United States, he was bound to act no part which could injure the nation; he was bound to keep the peace in regard to all nations with whom we are at peace. This is the law of nations; not an *ex post facto* law, but a law that was in existence long before Gideon Henfield existed.

But this was not all. "There are, also," the learned judge continued, "positive laws, existing previous to the offence committed, and expressly declared to be part of the supreme law of the land." He had in mind treaties, and he referred, among others, to the definitive treaty of peace with

[1] Francis Wharton, *State Trials* (Philadelphia, 1849), pp. 49, 84.

Great Britain, which declared, he stated, "that there shall be a firm and perpetual peace between His Britannic Majesty and the United States, and between the subjects of the one and the citizens of the other." [1] It was clearly the opinion of the court that Gideon Henfield had offended against the law of nations in general and in particular, and that, since the law of nations was acknowledged by the United States, he had committed "an offence against this country" and was "punishable by its laws."

A second illustration is that of a war vessel of a foreign belligerent country being fitted out within the United States. A year after the Gideon Henfield case the Neutrality Act, to which I have referred, was passed. Its provision on this phase of the question is that any person who, within the "waters of the United States," fitted out and armed or was knowingly "concerned in the furnishing, fitting out or arming of any ship or vessel" for employment "in the service of any foreign prince or state . . . with whom the United States are at peace," or who issued "a commission within the territory or jurisdiction of the United States for any ship or vessel to the intent that she may be employed as aforesaid," should, if convicted, "be adjudged guilty of a high misdemeanor, and shall be fined and imprisoned at the discretion of the court," the fine to be in no case "more than five thousand dollars" and the imprisonment not to "exceed three years. . . ." [2]

The statute further provided that a person engaged in augmenting the force of any armed vessel or any cruiser of a foreign country within the jurisdiction of the United States, the country to which it belongs being at peace with the United States, should "upon conviction be adjudged guilty of a misdemeanor," and should "be fined and imprisoned at the discretion of the court," with the further proviso that the fine should "not exceed one thousand dollars, nor the term of imprisonment be more than one year." [3]

It would be supposed that if any person within the jurisdiction of the United States were to be punished for enlisting in the crew of a foreign belligerent vessel, and if any individual were to be punished for issuing commissions within the United States, and if any individual were to be punished for augmenting the force of any ship, that any group of individuals setting on foot expeditions against the "territory or dominions of any foreign prince or state with whom the United States are at peace" [4] would likewise be fined; and such, indeed, was the case, the statute providing for this offense a fine not to "exceed three thousand dollars," and imprisonment for not more than three years. Nor should it astonish us, given the above provisions of the Neutrality Act, that captures made by a belligerent "within the waters of the United States or within a marine league of the coasts or shores thereof" [5] should be declared unlawful, as, indeed, they were.

And finally, the statute, to be complete, would need to define not merely

---

[1] Francis Wharton, *State Trials* (Philadelphia, 1849), p. 85.
[2] Act of June 5, 1794—An Act in addition to the act for the punishment of certain crimes against the United States, 1 Stat. 383, § 3.
[3] *Ibid.*, § 4.   [4] *Ibid.*, p. 384, § 5.   [5] *Ibid.*, p. 384, § 6.

the offense and the punishment, but the court in which the person or persons guilty of the offense should be tried.   It was to be the district court of the United States of the jurisdiction in which the offense was committed.[1]

It is to be observed that in all these provisions the offense is committed within the jurisdiction of the United States.   But if the same offense should be committed in a foreign country, the offense should be punishable by the laws of that country as in the case of the United States, and if the offense should not be so punished, it would be as a liability under international law, to be the subject of diplomatic negotiations, and, failing in them, to be submitted to an international tribunal.

Let us say a word of contraband and of blockade.   It is admitted to be a right of the citizens of each and every state under the customary law of nations to trade in certain articles, called contraband articles, which help a belligerent in prosecuting its real or alleged right under international law. But it is also the right of the belligerent to seize the commodities under certain conditions and to prevent the entry of a neutral vessel and cargo into a blockaded port of the enemy.   The carriage of contraband is permitted to the neutral, however, only if it has not been declared a punishable wrong in the proclamations of neutrality which the neutral states are accustomed to issue after the outbreak of a war.   Their citizens are warned in these proclamations that in carrying contraband and in seeking to enter a blockaded port, they do so at their peril.   When in the future the carriage of contraband or the running of blockades is made a legal wrong by international law, there will then be a municipal duty on the part of the neutral to provide a penalty for the offense in either case.

I have already referred to piracy, but it is here a last and crowning example.   It is robbery or theft committed by force upon the high seas.   The flag which the pirate vessel may fly is not regarded as that of any country; and such vessel has no protection from its flag, if it engage in an act of piracy, for piracy is an offense against each and every nation of the international community and the pirate is looked upon as an enemy of the human race.   Therefore it is that, wherever the act be committed, the pirate vessel coming into any port is subject to seizure and the crew liable to the punishment of death, which is the international punishment for the international crime of piracy.   This is an extreme example, in that any vessel guilty of piracy, without reference to the nationality of the vessel or of the equipment of the crew, may be proceeded against in any port of any nation to which vessel or crew is brought.

Is it not possible to assimilate to piracy an act which the nations have agreed should be treated as piracy?   We do not need to argue the question. It is not theoretical; it is practical, inasmuch as this very step was taken in the matter of belligerent attacks upon merchant vessels in the treaty signed

---

[1] For a judicial confirmation of this principle see Justice Johnson's opinion in behalf of a unanimous court in *United States* v. *Hudson,* 7 Cranch 32 (1812).

at Washington, February 6, 1922,[1] of which ratification was advised by the Senate of the United States on March 22 of the same year. The provision in question of this treaty, which assimilated to piracy acts in contravention "of the humane rules of existing law," was adopted by the Conference for the Limitation of Armament, held at Washington in 1922, upon the proposal, it should be said, of no less a person than Mr. Elihu Root.

Thus we have instances of municipal laws passed in order to punish violations of international law, whether they take place within the exclusive jurisdiction of the state in question or upon the high seas, outside of the exclusive jurisdiction of any state—as in the case of piracy, which, being an offense against humanity, is triable within any jurisdiction within which the vessel or the members of the piratical crew be found.

In the English-speaking world, crime is punishable within and according to the laws of the country where it is committed. Non-English-speaking countries also punish violations of their law which take place within a country according to the law of the particular country; but, as a general rule, the law follows their nationals, whithersoever they go, to such a degree that an offense against the law of their own country, although committed within a foreign jurisdiction, is punishable when the national returns to the homeland. But there is a tendency, even in the English-speaking world, to pass laws for the punishment of an increasing number of offenses committed in foreign parts, upon the national being found within the jurisdiction of the country whereof he is a subject or citizen.

* * *

Let us consider certain international cases which involved violations of the law of nations, and which gave rise to extended diplomatic negotiations, but which were fortunately settled without a resort to force. We may, indeed we should, begin with a case in which the United States violated international law to the detriment of Great Britain and the world at large. It is the *Trent* case,[2] almost as well known as the *Alabama* case.

Now the *Trent* was a British packet, and therefore a neutral ship, in the Civil War between the states of the American Union. It was a mail steamer, entirely neutral in its action, plying as it was on its regular voyage between two neutral ports, Vera Cruz (Mexico) and St. Thomas (Danish West

[1] Treaty relating to the use of submarines and noxious gases (Conferences on the Limitation of Armament, Washington, 1922), Art. III, p. 1608.

[2] On the *Trent* case see John Bassett Moore's *Digest of International Law* (Washington, 1906), vol. vii, pp. 768–779. Judge Moore observes (p. 775), that "the fullest and most satisfactory discussion of the *Trent case* is that given in the monograph of Dr. Heinrich Marquardsen, the preface to which is dated at Erlangen, February, 1862." The title of the monograph is *Der Trent-Fall*.

For Captain Wilkes' report, in defense of his conduct, to the Secretary of the Navy, written aboard the *San Jacinto*, "At sea, November 16, 1861," see Senate Ex. Doc. 1, 37th Cong., 2d Sess., vol. 3, p. 123.

For the protests of Great Britain and France, see Sen. Ex. Doc. 8, 37th Cong., 2d sess., vol. 4, pp. 2–16. The protest of Austria is to be found in Sen. Ex. Doc. 14, pp. 1–2, and of Prussia in Sen. Ex. Doc. 18, pp. 1–3.

Indies), by way of Havana.   It had aboard among its passengers two civil agents of the Southern Confederacy (Messrs. Mason and Slidell), the one of Virginia, the other of Louisiana, both members of the Confederacy, who were on their way to St. Thomas to embark on a British steamer for South-ampton, England.   As passengers on the *Trent* they were on a British, and therefore neutral, steamer, sailing under the British flag, on a scheduled voyage between neutral points.   The *San Jacinto* was a man-of-war of the United States, commanded by a "man of war," Charles Wilkes, who nearly precipitated a war between the two countries.   He hailed the *Trent* on November 8, 1861, had it boarded, and removed Messrs. Mason and Slidell, taking them aboard his vessel and landing them in Boston harbor, where he found himself a popular hero, with his digestion threatened by banquets in his honor.

As confirmed by his official reports of the affair,[1] Captain Wilkes had acted without orders from his government, indeed without knowledge of the authorities in Washington.[2]   Each government involved found itself in an embarrassing position.   What Captain Wilkes had done was in accordance with the principles of international law as laid down by my Lord Stowell in his prize court decisions and, therefore, in accordance with British practice,[3] of which the United States had formerly and repeatedly complained.   There-fore, the Government of the United States after the event could not well approve Captain Wilkes' action, without at the same time accepting that British policy, which had been one of the causes of the War of 1812.

The Government of Great Britain, on its part, was no doubt inwardly pleased that, in opposing Captain Wilkes' action, it was upholding the con-tention of the United States in earlier days, when the American Government had insisted that American merchant vessels, in a war in which the United States were neutral, should not be subject to visit and search, and the re-moval of civilians from American merchantmen.   President Lincoln himself warned against inconsistency:

We must stick to American principles concerning the rights of neutrals.   We fought Great Britain for insisting, by theory and practice, on the right to do precisely what Captain

---

[1] Gideon Welles, "The Capture and Release of Mason and Slidell," *The Galaxy* (New York, 1873), Vol. XV, p. 647.

[2] Ephraim Douglass Adams, *Great Britain and the American Civil War* (New York and London, 1925), Vol. I, p. 205.   Secretary Seward to Mr. Adams, November 27, 1861, in John G. Nicolay and John Hay, *Abraham Lincoln* (New York, 1890), Vol. 5, p. 32.   In further reference to this point, see the statement of Miss Slidell, one of the *Trent* passengers, sum-marized on p. 517 of the *Proceedings of the Massachusetts Historical Society* (1911–1912), Vol. 45 (Richard Henry Dana's paper on "The Trent Affair—An Aftermath"), that "the Ameri-can officer who boarded the *Trent* took pains to state that the commander of the *San Jacinto* had no instructions from his Government, but was acting on his own responsibility."

[3] See letter of Lord Palmerston to Mr. Delane, editor of the London *Times*, Nov. 11, 1861, involving the very point at issue, in which his Lordship admitted that the right of a belliger-ent "to stop and search any neutral not being a ship of war, and being found on the high seas and being suspected of carrying enemy's despatches" was "according to the principles of international law laid down in our courts by Lord Stowell, and practised and enforced by us."   E. D. Adams, *op. cit.*, p. 208.   See also *The Galaxy*, above cited, p. 650, column 1, lines 3–5.

Wilkes has done. If Great Britain shall now protest against the act, and demand their release, we must give them up, apologize for the act as a violation of our doctrines, and thus forever bind her over to keep the peace in relation to neutrals, and so acknowledge that she has been wrong for sixty years.[1]

What was to be done? Her Majesty, Queen Victoria, and the Prince Consort were opposed to any war with the United States. Secretary Seward, in behalf of the American Government, declared, in what is described as "one of his chief literary triumphs," [2] that Captain Wilkes had acted on his own responsibility and that his action was not approved; and likewise in behalf of the government, he expressed regret at the incident.[3] Great Britain was willing to and did accept the *amende honorable*. The two commissioners were therefore returned to British custody. But their usefulness, as it turned out, had ended.

The result of the incident was that the governments of the two countries admitted in principle that the early practice of Great Britain and the unauthorized action of Captain Wilkes were opposed to the principles of international law.

If this were all, we should not be citing the incident on this occasion. Of course, Great Britain had the right to protest, and it was in our interest as well as Great Britain's that Her Majesty's Government did so. But Prussia protested, Austria protested, and France protested. Each was right; and every member of the international community would have been right if each had protested. For if it was a right of Great Britain, as a neutral, to protest the unneutral action of the United States, it was the right of each and every member of the international community to protest.[4] It was indeed a threefold right: a right in behalf of Great Britain as the nation directly in-

---

[1] Nicolay and Hay, *op. cit.*, pp. 25, 26. President Lincoln was in the habit of referring to Messrs. Mason and Slidell as calculated "to be white elephants."

[2] *Ibid.*, p. 38. Concerning this document, the authors say: "That long and remarkably able document must be read in full, both to understand the wide range of the subject which he treated and the clearness and force of his language and arguments. It constitutes one of his chief literary triumphs. There is room here only to indicate the conclusions arrived at in his examination. First, he held that the four persons seized and their dispatches were contraband of war; second, that Captain Wilkes had a right by the law of nations to detain and search the *Trent;* third, that he exercised the right in a lawful proper manner; fourth, that he had a right to capture the contraband found. The real issue of the case centered in the fifth question: 'Did Captain Wilkes exercise the right of capturing the contraband in conformity with the law of nations?' Reciting the deficiency of recognized rules on this point, Mr. Seward held that only by taking the vessel before a prize court could the existence of contraband be lawfully established; and that Captain Wilkes having released the vessel from capture, the necessary judicial examination was prevented, and the capture left unfinished or abandoned."

[3] See comment of Secretary Welles, *Diary of Gideon Welles* (Boston, 1911), Vol. I, p. 299.

[4] The correspondence of Russia and Italy on the *Trent* case is published in Sen. Ex. Docs. 22 (pp. 1–3) and 30 (pp. 1–3), respectively. From these documents it will be seen that Russia expresses its satisfaction over the maintenance, instead of the repudiation, of the early American doctrine; while Italy, also expressing its satisfaction at the peaceful solution reached through the conciliatory attitude of the United States, stated its own attachment to the freedom of the seas, and added that "we hesitated to believe that it [the Government of the United States] desired to change its character all at once and become the champion of theories which history has shown to be calamitous, and which public opinion has condemned forever."

jured; the right of Prussia, of Austria, and of France as subject to a prospective injury; and the right of each and every one directly or prospectively injured to protest not only in behalf of the law common to each of the neutral nations, but also in behalf of the international community of which each was a member.

If the ministers of foreign affairs of Prussia, Austria and France were today to contemplate such action, they would be able to invoke the unimpeachable authority of a great American statesman, Elihu Root, himself once a Secretary of State:

> . . . it follows necessarily that when one sovereign state is dealing not with its internal affairs but with its international relations and violates the rule of right as against another equal and independent state, all other equally independent states have a right to insist that the international rule shall be observed, and such insistence is not interfering with the quarrels of others but is an assertion of their own rights.   In each case every state must be guided by its own circumstances and interests in determining how far it will go in supporting its interference.   There can, however, be no doubt of the international right to interfere in behalf of the maintenance of the law.[1]

Let us hold the scales of justice even and now take a case in which Great Britain violated international law to the detriment of the United States and the world at large.

The classic example of this phase of the question is that of the *Alabama*, a cruiser built in a British shipyard in Liverpool, at the request of agents of the Government of the Confederate States of America, and to be used by the authorities of the Confederate States to commit hostilities against the United States.   The case of the *Alabama* is not only the classic case, but the arbitration is the classic arbitration of the nineteenth century.   The case was in a way an accident, very unfortunate for Great Britain.   The arbitration, however, was in the interest of Great Britain, as well as of the United States and of the world at large, because it showed that arbitration might stop the hand of war in a case which threatened to plunge the two English-speaking nations into what we may call a fratricidal, if not a civil, war.

The case was, as I have said, accidental.   The American Minister, Charles Francis Adams, of the classic Adams family of the United States, had informed the British Government that a certain vessel (No. 290) was being built in behalf of the Confederate Government in the British shipyard of Lairds at Liverpool.   Her Majesty's principal Secretary of State for Foreign Affairs, the Earl of Russell, formerly and affectionately known as Lord John Russell, was unwilling to undertake the action which Mr. Adams requested, namely, to take steps so that the vessel should not be permitted to depart from British waters.   However, he recognized, and well he might, the gravity of the affair and submitted the question in the usual course to the Queen's

---

[1] From an address of April 27, 1916, before the American Society of International Law on "The Declaration of the Rights and Duties of Nations of the American Institute of International Law," published in *Addresses on International Law Subjects*, by Elihu Root (1916), pp. 421, 422.

Advocate, Sir John Harding.   Now the Queen's Advocate happened to be mentally incapacitated, a fact which his devoted wife concealed from the authorities, so that the request for the information lay unanswered upon his desk.[1]   Finally, when Mr. Adams persisted in his statement that the vessel was being built for the Confederate Government and that it would soon take the seas, his Lordship bestirred himself, and, learning of Sir John Harding's situation, submitted the question to the other law officers of the Crown, the Attorney General, Sir William Atherton, and the then Solicitor General, Sir Roundell Palmer, later, as Lord Selborne, to be Lord High Chancellor, who advised that the vessel be seized and not permitted to depart from British jurisdiction.   However, the vessel had that very morning— July 28, 1862—taken the seas, which fact Lord Russell should have known and prevented.   Mr. Adams knew that the vessel was to depart and His Lordship, with better means of knowledge at his disposal, should also have known and should have prevented its leaving British jurisdiction.

In addition, the shipbuilding Lairds had under construction for the Confederate States certain vessels known as "iron rams," "designed to raise the blockade" of the Southern ports.   In September, 1863, the rams were about to put to sea, Lord Russell announcing that the British authorities "advise that they cannot interfere in any way with these vessels."   Whereupon Mr. Adams countered with: "My lord, it would be superfluous in me to point out to your Lordship that this is war." [2]   The "rams" did not sail.

The tension produced by the "unneutral" conduct of Great Britain in the matter of Confederate vessels was the source of immense irritation in the United States, and irritation in Great Britain because of the irritation in America.   Incidents such as these all too often generate war.

Now it so happened—and this is the fortunate part of the incident—that Mr. Gladstone later became Prime Minister, and he accepted the suggestion of a peaceful settlement in the form of arbitration by an arbitral tribunal. Thus it was that the treaty of May 8, 1871, in its first article, provided "that all the said claims, growing out of acts committed by the aforesaid vessels, and generally known as the 'Alabama Claims,' shall be referred to a tribunal of arbitration to be composed of five Arbitrators," one to be "named" by the President of the United States; one by Her Britannic Majesty; one by His Majesty the King of Italy; one by the President of the Swiss Confederation; and finally, one by His Majesty the Emperor of Brazil.[3]

It is to be observed that there were three "Majesties" and two "Presidents"; but we of the American Republic are happy to be able to say that the decision was in behalf of the "presidential" claimant.   The tribunal was

[1] See John Bassett Moore, *Principles of American Diplomacy* (New York, 1918), pp. 50, 51.
[2] Charles Francis Adams, "Memoir of Hon. Charles Francis Adams, LL.D.," in *Proceedings of the Massachusetts Historical Society*, Second Series (Boston, 1900), Vol. XIII, p. 205.
[3] *Treaties, Conventions, International Acts, Protocols, and Agreements between the United States of America and Other Powers*, 1776–1909, compiled by Wm. M. Malloy (Washington, 1910), Vol. I, p. 701.

to meet at Geneva, which it did, on December 15, 1871, and the claims were to be decided "by a majority of all the Arbitrators." [1]   The *Alabama* case was unanimously decided, although the British arbitrator, Sir Alexander Cockburn, then Lord Chief Justice of the Queen's Bench, rendered a separate opinion assigning separate reasons from those stated in the majority opinion.

The contention of the United States was that the conduct of Great Britain was in violation of the law of nations.   This, Great Britain denied.   As a result of discussion, the representatives of the two countries agreed that—

In deciding the matters submitted to the Arbitrators, they shall be governed by the follow-ing three rules, which are agreed upon by the high contracting parties as rules to be taken as applicable to the case, and by such principles of international law not inconsistent there-with as the Arbitrators shall determine to have been applicable to the case. [2]

The three rules were:

A neutral Government is bound—

First, to use due diligence to prevent the fitting out, arming, or equipping, within its jurisdiction, of any vessel which it has reasonable ground to believe is intended to cruise or to carry on war against a Power with which it is at peace; and also to use like diligence to pre-vent the departure from its jurisdiction of any vessel intended to cruise or carry on war as above, such vessel having been specially adapted, in whole or in part, within such jurisdic-tion, to warlike use.

Secondly, not to permit or suffer either belligerent to make use of its ports or waters as the base of naval operations against the other, or for the purpose of the renewal or augmentation of military supplies or arms, or the recruitment of men.

Thirdly, to exercise due diligence in its own ports and waters, and, as to all persons within its jurisdiction, to prevent any violation of the foregoing obligations and duties. [3]

The British Government did not, as already mentioned, accept these rules as rules of international law, and "Her Britannic Majesty," so runs the treaty, "commanded her High Commissioners and Plenipotentiaries to declare that Her Majesty's Government cannot assent to the foregoing rules as a statement of principles of international law which were in force at the time when the claims mentioned in Article I arose." However, "Her Majesty's Government, in order to evince its desire of strengthening the friendly relations between the two countries and of making satisfactory provision for the future," agreed that, in deciding the claims, "the Arbitra-tors should assume that Her Majesty's Government had undertaken to act upon the principles set forth in these rules." [4]   By so doing, Great Britain accepted in advance an adverse decision.

But if those rules were not rules at the time, they were to become so, and they are to be the rules of the future, for the high contracting parties agreed "to observe these rules as between themselves in future, and to bring them to the knowledge of other maritime Powers, and to invite them to accede to them."   They have acceded to them in substance if not in form. [5]

---

[1] *Ibid.*, Art. II, p. 702.   [2] *Ibid.*, Art. VI, p. 703.   [3] *Ibid.*   [4] *Ibid.*
[5] See Convention (XIII) concerning the Rights and Duties of Neutral Powers in Naval War, signed at The Hague, October 18, 1907—Articles 5, 6, 8, 18, and 25.

The importance of the *Alabama* case lies in the fact that if there be no international law upon which the parties are agreed, they can make the law for the case, so that through their initiative the rules which had not been declared to form a part of international law may, as the rule of right reason, become international law by the agreement of the nations and thus become the municipal law of each and every country so accepting them.

The tribunal . . . has arrived at the decision embodied in the present award. . . .

And whereas the circumstances . . . were of a nature to call for the exercise on the part of Her Britannic Majesty's government of all possible solicitude for the observance of the rights and the duties involved in the proclamation of neutrality issued by Her Majesty on the 13th day of May, 1861;

And whereas the effects of a violation of neutrality committed by means of the construction, equipment, and armament of a vessel are not done away with by any commission which the government of the belligerent power, benefited by the violation of neutrality, may afterward have granted to that vessel, and the ultimate step by which the offense is completed, cannot be admissible as a ground for the absolution of the offender, nor can the consummation of his fraud become the means of establishing his innocence;

And whereas the privilege of exterritoriality accorded to vessels of war has been admitted into the law of nations, not as an absolute right, but solely as a proceeding founded on the principle of courtesy and mutual deference between different nations, and therefore can never be appealed to for the protection of acts done in violation of neutrality;

And whereas the absence of a previous notice cannot be regarded as a failure in any consideration required by the law of nations, in those cases in which a vessel carries with it its own condemnation;

And whereas, in order to impart to any supplies of coal a character inconsistent with the second rule, prohibiting the use of neutral ports or waters, as a base of naval operations for a belligerent, it is necessary that said supplies should be connected with special circumstances of time, of person, or of place, which may combine to give them such character; . . .[1]

It will be observed that the above "whereases" were framed by the tribunal in such a way as to lay down the general principles applicable to all the violations of neutality with respect to the Confederate vessel involved. The tribunal now proceeded to apply them to all of the vessels. But as we are interested at present only in the vessel which has given its name to the arbitration, I quote here merely the award in its behalf:

And whereas, with respect to the vessel called the *Alabama*, it clearly results from all the facts relative to the construction of the ship at first designated by the number '290' in the port of Liverpool, and its equipment and armament in the vicinity of Terceira through the agency of the vessels called the *Agrippina* and the *Bahama*, dispatched from Great Britain to that end, that the British government failed to use due diligence in the performance of its neutral obligations; and especially that it omitted, notwithstanding the warnings and official representations made by the diplomatic agents of the United States during the construction of the said number '290,' to take in due time any effective measures of prevention, and that those orders which it did give at last, for the detention of the vessel, were issued so late that their execution was not practicable;

And whereas, after the escape of that vessel, the measures taken for its pursuit and arrest were so imperfect as to lead to no result, and therefore cannot be considered sufficient to release Great Britain from the responsibility already incurred;

[1] The *Alabama* case, cited above, p. 18, note 1.

And whereas, in spite of the violations of the neutrality of Great Britain committed by the '290', this same vessel, later known as the Confederate cruiser *Alabama*, was on several occasions freely admitted to the ports of colonies of Great Britain, instead of being proceeded against as it ought to have been in any and every port within British jurisdiction in which it might have been found;

And whereas the government of Her Britannic Majesty cannot justify itself for a failure in due diligence on the plea of insufficiency of the legal means of action which it possessed:

Four of the arbitrators, for the reasons above assigned, and the fifth, for reasons separately assigned by him,

Are of opinion—

That Great Britain has in this case failed, by omission, to fulfill the duties prescribed in the first and the third of the rules established by the sixth article of the treaty of Washington.[1]

It is not necessary to say a further word in this connection other than that, as international law was law, as such it measured the right of the United States and the duty of Great Britain, and that the failure of Great Britain to take the necessary preventive measures and to provide judicial remedies, rendered that country liable for a violation of international law; and that the lack of a municipal statute to that effect was no excuse before an international tribunal.

* * *

There was an aftermath to the *Alabama* case which, although the judgment of a national court, is hardly less important than the award of an international tribunal, and it is to be observed that the opinion of a unanimous court was delivered in the case of the *United States* v. *Arjona*[2] by the same Morrison R. Waite, then Chief Justice, who had with great distinction argued the case of the *Alabama* for the United States before the Alabama Tribunal; and, curiously enough, the case in the Supreme Court, as in the arbitral tribunal, turned upon the question of "due diligence," applicable alike in a national as well as in an international tribunal.

The facts of the *Arjona* case are simple. A law of the United States of May 16, 1884,[3] had been passed by the Congress "to prevent and punish the counterfeiting within the United States of notes, bonds, and other securities of foreign Governments." That statute had been violated within the jurisdiction of the United States by one Ramon Arjona. He was tried for having violated this statute within the jurisdiction of the United States, to the detriment of Colombia. The Federal Court before which he was tried was divided in opinion, and the case was certified to the Supreme Court of the United States. The question upon which the lower court divided was the constitutionality of the statute which the defendant had violated.

The Supreme Court held that the statute in question was constitutional, and that, indeed, it was the duty of the United States to pass the act in question, and that if the Government of the United States had not passed the act, it would have been remiss in its duty toward the injured nation and

---

[1] *Ibid.*, pp. 148, 149.   [2] 120 U. S. 479 (1887).
[3] 23 Stat. 22 (1884), 18 U. S. Code, § 270 (1926).

toward every other nation of the international community.   After citing various articles of the Constitution, the Chief Justice, speaking for the Court, announced its opinion that—

All official intercourse between a state and foreign nations is prevented, and exclusive authority for that purpose given to the United States.   The national government is in this way made responsible to foreign nations for all violations by the United States of their international obligations, and because of this, Congress is expressly authorized 'to define and punish . . . offences against the law of nations.'

What then, is this law of nations, which the Government of the United States would have violated, had it not passed the act in question?   "The law of nations"—the Chief Justice said, speaking, as stated, for a unanimous court—"requires every national government to use 'due diligence' to prevent a wrong being done within its own dominion to another nation with which it is at peace, or to the people thereof; and because of this, the obligation of one nation to punish those who, within its own jurisdiction, counterfeit the money of another nation, has long been recognized."   It is, indeed, interesting to learn from such an authoritative source that the obligation was of long standing, but the importance of the statement lies in the fact that a rule of international law requires each and every member of the international community to enact a municipal statute for the protection of a rule of the law of nations, just as the *Alabama* case, in which Chief Justice Waite had been counsel, decided not merely that the failure to do so, but that the lack of due diligence, rendered Great Britain liable in damages; that is to say, every rule of the law of nations has *in esse* or *in posse* a municipal sanction.   Let us follow the Chief Justice in his friendly invasion of the domain of international law:

Vattel,—he says—in his Law of Nations, which was first printed at Neuchatel in 1758, and was translated into English and published in England in 1760, uses this language: 'From the principles thus laid down, it is easy to conclude, that if one nation counterfeits the money of another, or if she allows and protects false coiners who presume to do it, she does that nation an injury.'

The Chief Justice here pauses to speak in his own behalf:

When this was written money was the chief thing of this kind that needed protection, but still it was added: 'There is another custom more modern, and of no less use to commerce than the establishment of coin, namely, *exchange*, or the traffic of bankers, by means of which a merchant remits immense sums from one end of the world to the other, at very trifling expense, and, if he pleases, without risk.'

Vattel himself penetrates the domain still farther, accompanied by the learned Chief Justice:

'For the same reason that sovereigns are obliged'—Vattel says—'to protect commerce, they are obliged to support this custom, by good laws, in which every merchant, whether citizen or foreigner, may find security.'

If commerce is to be protected by a nation, and laws are to be passed for that purpose by every nation, we have in these few lines a duty of due diligence which encircles the world.

So much for the law; now as to its application to the United States.

"No nation can be more interested in this question than the United States,"—the Chief Justice later continues—the meaning of which is that the United States can require of the other nations of the world that due diligence be used in order to protect their money, "their own securities, and those of the states, the cities, and the public corporations, whose interests abroad they alone have the power to guard against foreign national neglect, [which] are found on sale in the principal money markets of Europe." "But"—he continues, applying the rule of law to the United States—"if the United States can require this of another, that other may require it of them, because international obligations are of necessity reciprocal in their nature." For he adds that, "the right, if it exists at all, is given by the law of nations, and what is law for one is, under the same circumstances, law for the other." Therefore, he continues, "a right secured by the law of nations to a nation, or its people, is one the United States, as the representatives of this nation, are bound to protect. Consequently, a law which is necessary and proper to afford this protection is one that Congress may enact. . . . Therefore the United States must have the power to pass it and enforce it themselves, or be unable to perform a duty which they may owe to another nation, and which the law of nations has imposed on them as part of their international obligations."

It is to be observed that the duty does not arise by virtue of the municipal law of the United States. The duty arises from the law of nations—a law superior to municipal law, including in this category the Constitution of the United States which, to the world at large, is a domestic matter. And the judgment in the *Arjona* case is a solemn asseveration on the part of the Supreme Court of the United States that the law of nations is not a law which we accept, but a law which is "imposed" upon us and which we must protect; for, if we do not, we cannot invoke the rules of international law in our own benefit, and while we would not cease to be a member of the international community, we, nevertheless, would not be considered as a member in good standing.

We might well be content to rest our case upon these statements of the Chief Justice, which are also those of his brethren; for the complete reasoning of the Court requiring due diligence in enacting municipal legislation to protect a rule of the law of nations, is the contribution which the *Arjona* case makes to the law of the international community.

However, there is another phase of the case no less worthy of our attention. By Article I, section 8, clause 10 of the Constitution, the Congress is not merely impliedly, but expressly authorized "to define and punish . . . offences against the law of nations." This authorization does not *make* the

law of nations a part of our law; it *recognizes* the existence of the law of nations as a part of our law without action on our part, the law being—again to quote Chief Justice Waite—"imposed" upon the United States from their inception, as upon every state of the international community.   Indeed, the law of nations, existing before the birth of the United States, became "imposed" upon us the moment the United States came into being. It was not created by the United States; it was not adopted by the United States; it could not be adopted because it was already the law of the United States *ex jure necessitatis;* and it cannot be abrogated by the United States because it was not made by the United States.   Therefore, the United States cannot create international law; the most it can do is to define and to enforce it; but the expression "to define" international law is in itself a recognition of its existence, and the definition, it may be said, is only to make that express which is implicit.   But that does not, indeed cannot, mean that the definition which the Government of the United States may make of international law is acceptable to the other nations.   If it be correct, it is binding, not because it is the act of the United States, but because the definition of international law made or proposed by the United States is in accordance with, to use Victoria's phrase, "a consensus of the greater part of the whole world, especially in behalf of the common good of all."

This is indeed much, but it is not all.   The statute creating a liability within the jurisdiction of the United States does not need to mention that it is passed to render effective the law of nations, because the law of nations is the law of the United States, whether it be so stated or not.   As this phase of the case arose, it was considered and likewise decided by the Supreme Court. Let us, however, allow the Chief Justice to speak in behalf of the Court, numbering his questions and answers in the paragraph of the opinion dealing with this phase which is, as it were, a link in the chain of the argument.

1. Whether, in enacting a statute to define and punish an offence against the law of nations, it is necessary, in order 'to define' the offence, that it be declared in the statute itself to be 'an offence against the law of nations.'

2. This statute defines the offence, and if the thing made punishable is one which the United States are required by their international obligations to use due diligence to prevent, it is an offence against the law of nations.

3. Such being the case, there is no more need of declaring in the statute that it is such an offence, than there would be in any other criminal statute to declare that it was enacted to carry into execution any other particular power vested by the Constitution in the Government of the United States.

4. Whether the offence as defined is an offence against the law of nations depends on the thing done, not on any declaration to that effect by Congress.

This is a short and weighty sentence implying that in matters international the Congress of the United States is a mere legislature of the international community for the enactment of a municipal statute in order to create a municipal sanction for the protection, or redress of a violation, of a rule of the law of nations.

5. As has already been seen, it was incumbent on the United States as a nation to use due diligence to prevent any injury to another nation or its people by counterfeiting its money, or its public or *quasi* public securities.

6. This statute was enacted as a means to that end, that is to say, as a means of performing a duty which had been cast on the United States by the law of nations, and it was clearly appropriate legislation for that purpose.

A break in the quotation must be made to call attention to the phrase "cast on the United States," not "made by the United States."

7. Upon its face, therefore, it [the statute] defines an offence against the law of nations as clearly as if Congress had in express terms so declared.

Seven is said to be the perfect number, and the decision of the Supreme Court in the *Arjona* case can be said to be equally perfect.

Indeed it would almost seem that *United States* v. *Arjona* was, as it were, a case not actually arising in practice, but stated by the Court in order to show the students of international law that the law of nations exists without an affirmative act on the part of the respective countries; that this law of nations so imposed, "casts" a duty upon every civilized nation to enact municipal laws to protect a right under the law of nations, thus complying with a duty, not only of the particular country in question, but a duty under international law; that a failure so to comply, renders the nation so failing liable in damages to the nation injured; and that the failure to use due diligence either in passing the municipal law, or in preventing the violation of international law, renders the nation liable under the law of nations, because the municipal statute should have been in existence at the time of the injury—for liability arises even though a subsequent statute be enacted. The injury looks to the past; the statute to the future.

This was the predicament in which England found itself in the reign of Queen Anne, and this was why the passage of a statute and a remedy under the statute, were not regarded as a compliance with the duty which England owed to the Russian Ambassador at the very moment of his arrest. The injuries of the past are not cured by subsequent statute.

To state it all in a word: International law should be, and is today, we may happily say, the law of every nation in the civilized world. It may have, and in some instances does have, a specific and international sanction. But whether or not it has such a sanction, it nevertheless involves the duty on the part of each nation to pass appropriate and adequate laws providing a municipal remedy for any and every violation of international law, whether in peace or in war, within its jurisdiction—that is to say, within its own territory where its jurisdiction is exclusive, or on the high seas where jurisdiction is common to all nations. But the consideration of this duty raises an important issue. A sanction cannot be provided for any law unless that law is properly formulated—at least in general terms.

Now the formulation and adequate statement of international law can only mean the codification of international law—a world code for a world

law in clear and unmistakable but general terms—leaving to each nation the duty to enact municipal statutes most apt, in its opinion, to comply in full measure with its obligations under the law of nations.

"From all that has been said," to quote again, and finally, the language of Victoria, "a corollary may be inferred, namely: that international law has not only the force of a pact and agreement among men, but also the force of a law; for the world as a whole, being in a way one single State, has the power to create laws that are just and fitting for all persons, as are the rules of international law. Consequently, it is clear that they who violate these international rules, whether in peace or in war, commit a mortal sin; moreover, in the gravest matters, such as the inviolability of ambassadors, it is not permissible for one country to refuse to be bound by international law, the latter having been established by the authority of the whole world."

PART II

FRANCISCO SUÁREZ

Strictly and absolutely speaking, only that which is a measure of rectitude, viewed absolutely—and consequently, only that which is a right and virtuous rule—can be called law.

The eternal law has first place, on account of its dignity and excellence, and because it is the source and origin of all laws.

Natural law is the first system whereby the eternal law has been applied or made known to us. . . .

The natural law is made known to men in a twofold way, first through natural reason, and secondly, through the law of the Decalogue written on the Mosaic tablets. . . .

The *jus gentium* is the most closely related to the natural law.

All the precepts written by God in the hearts of men, pertain to the natural law, a fact which may be gathered from the words of Paul [*Romans*, chap. ii (vs. 14–15)]: and all precepts which may clearly be inferred by reason from natural principles are written in human hearts; therefore, all such precepts pertain to the natural law.

The commands relating to the restitution of the property of another, or the return of a deposit, or observing good faith, to telling the truth, and to similar matters . . . pertain in the highest degree to the province of the natural law.

It should be further noted that, among the precepts of natural law, there are certain ones, dealing with pacts, agreements, or obligations, which are introduced through the will of men. Such are the laws relating to the observance of vows and of human promises, whether these be made in simple form or confirmed by oath; and the same is true of other contracts, according to the particular characteristics of each; and true, also, of the rights or duties arising therefrom.

In the case of any contract or commercial agreement . . . the observance of the contract after it has been made . . . pertains to the natural law. . . .

Likewise, treaties of peace and truces may be placed under the head of the *jus gentium* in the strict sense of the term; not in so far as relates to the obligation to observe them after they are made, since this obligation pertains rather to the natural law; but in so far as [offers to make] such treaties should be heeded, and not refused, when duly presented, and for a reasonable cause. . . .

With regard . . . to peace, truces and ambassadors, . . . all the [rules] on these points have their foundation in some human agreement, in which both the power to contract [a treaty or convention] and the obligation arising from that treaty or convention and demanding good faith and justice, have regard to the law of nature. Only the exercise [of these powers] may be termed a part of the *jus gentium* owing to the accord of all nations with respect to the exercise of such faculties, generally speaking. And this actual use [of the powers in question] is the effect of law, and not law itself; for the law under discussion does not spring from such use; on the contrary, the use has its source in the law.

It remains that we explain in what manner the computation of the "major portion" should be made, or of what persons it is composed. There is a general agreement on this point, that there should be reckoned in this number only such persons as can give consent to a legal custom. All infants are, therefore, excluded, and all persons mentally defective. Some would also exclude women entirely, on the grounds that they can exercise no legislative authority. Among men, they exclude all below the age of twenty-five years. However, I cannot find any basis in law or any justification in reason for the exclusion of the last two groups.—*De Legibus ac Deo Legislatore.*

PART II

FRANCISCO SUÁREZ

HIS PHILOSOPHY OF LAW AND OF SANCTIONS

Wherein does Francisco Suárez differ from Francisco de Vitoria?   If they do not differ, we can not claim that Suárez had a hand in the founding of the modern law of nations; he could at most only be considered as confirming what Victoria had already proclaimed.   He did indeed confirm what Victoria had stated; but that is not all.   He has added a something, and that something gave to the conception of the great Dominican nothing more nor less than a philosophy of law and of the modern law of nations.   Indeed, this is so evident that Dr. Jan Kosters,[1] a distinguished countryman of Grotius and a judge of the Supreme Court of the Netherlands, who has devoted himself to this problem, says that after the labors of Suárez the fruit of the international tree was ripe for plucking.   And we in our own behalf have ventured to add, on a former occasion, that it was the hand of a Netherlander, the hand of Grotius, that plucked it.[2]

Here we have a threefold relationship.   First the expounder; second the philosopher; and third, the compiler, or, if that term be looked upon as belittling, the purveyor of the ideas of others, or, rather, a popularizer in the best sense of the word.   And as a popularizer the services of Grotius to international law should never be overlooked.   The modern law of nations of which Victoria was the expounder, Suárez the philosopher, and Grotius the systematizer, is the contribution of what we may call, and indeed must call, the Spanish School of International Law.   For if Grotius was not a Spaniard by blood, he was a Spaniard in his conception of international law, and so far as the basic principles of his system are concerned, he was indubitably a member of the Spanish School.

The contributions of Suárez to the epoch-making exposition of Victoria are the analysis and definition of the general and specific kinds of law, their origin, their nature, their various forms or categories: the law natural in its several manifestations, the law of the state in its individual capacity, and the law of the states in their international capacity—in other words, the law of nations.

Both Victoria and Suárez were churchmen, and, in the highest and best sense of the word, they were theologians.   They were also jurists, because

[1] J. Kosters, "Fondements du Droit des Gens," published in the *Bibliotheca Visseriana* (Leyden, 1925), Vol. IV, p. 32.
[2] "Suárez and the International Community," *Addresses in Commemoration of His Contribution to International Law and Politics* (Catholic University of America, Washington, 1933), pp. 45–6.

the conception of theology of that day was an all-pervasive science embracing the conduct of men and women.[1]

Victoria was a practical man as well as a theorist, and a profound student of law in its various aspects. But when he found himself face to face with the American problems thrust upon his country by the western voyage of Columbus, he deemed it his duty to furnish a solution, and in furnishing the solution, he dealt with conclusions rather than with the premises leading to such conclusions. With the solution his work was complete; his task was finished. Yet even if we accept the conclusions and the reasoning by which they could be applied, not merely to a single concrete case, but to all concrete cases of a like nature, when and as they might present themselves, we still would need a philosophy which would justify and integrate the abstract principles behind the conclusions. This philosophy was the contribution of Suárez, although it may not have been his conscious purpose to complete theoretically what Victoria had begun practically.

If it may not be said that Victoria passed the torch of the new learning in matters international to the hand of Suárez, there was, nevertheless, an interval of but two years between the demise of the founder of the modern law of nations and the birth of him who was, to reiterate what can not too often be stated, to furnish law with its indispensable elements, and to state and define the different kinds of law, assigning each to its place, in such a way as to leave as his legacy to the world a law with a philosophy and a philosophy of law. Although Suárez never stood in the presence of the *maestro*, he studied at Salamanca and grew up in its noble traditions. St. Thomas Aquinas had become, as it were, through Victoria, the patron saint of the university, so that Suárez lived, in very fact, his impressionable years in an atmosphere absent elsewhere—the atmosphere of Victoria, enlarged and enriched by the spirit of Aquinas. This atmosphere of Victoria was very real, because the doctrines which he had developed and taught during the twenty years of his professorate at Salamanca were in turn professed with the earnestness of disciples by those who had sat at the feet of the master. And truly it may be said that these doctrines not merely entered

---

[1] The view of Victoria is expressed in the words of his Reading *De Potestate Civili*, quoted on a previous page, but worth repeating here: "The duties and functions of the theologian extend over a field so vast, that no argument, no discussion, no text, seem alien to the practice and purpose of theology. And this may account for the fact that the lack of able and sound theologians is as great as—not to say greater than—the lack of orators which is mentioned by Cicero, and which he explains by saying that men who are distinguished and skilled in every science and in all the arts are very rare. Theology, indeed, is the first of all those sciences and studies which the Greeks call θεολογία." Francisco de Vitoria, *De Potestate Civili*, a relectio dated Christmas, 1528. Latin Text, Simon's Edition of the *Relectiones Morales*, Cologne and Frankfort (1696).

Suárez, in the Preface to his *De Legibus*, expresses a somewhat similar view in different language: "For just as theologians should ponder concerning God for many other reasons, so also should they ponder concerning Him, for this reason: that He is the final end toward Whom rational creatures tend and in Whom their sole felicity consists. It follows, then, that sacred doctrine has this final end in view, and that it also sets forth the way to attain that end; since God is not only the end and, as it were, the goal, towards which all intellectual creatures are drawn, but also the cause whereby the goal is reached."

into, but were indeed the very foundation of what was to be known, in centuries to come, as the "Spanish School of International Law."

And so it happened that, when Suárez himself was ready to add his incomparable contribution to the Spanish School, he found a law of nations already in existence, not wholly lacking in philosophy—for none can deny that Victoria was a philosopher as well as a jurist—but nevertheless lacking a complete philosophical development.

The philosophy of Victoria was, however, for an occasion, or rather to bring a concrete situation—arising from the discovery of the New World—within the law of Christendom, thus universalizing it; whereas the purpose of Suárez was to state the law universal and its elements in the abstract, with sufficient reference to concrete instances to give it a substance and a body. With Victoria, the philosophy of law was subordinated to its application; with Suárez, the *desideratum* was the creation of a philosophy which would permeate not merely one form of law but all law, and would therefore apply not to a single, but to every concrete situation. Each, as it were, stands by himself; each is independent of the other; but together, through the combination of the concrete and the abstract, they gave, to nation and to nations, law and its philosophy.

Victoria's reputation as an international lawyer depends upon his application of the general principles of justice in relation to the one great concrete fact of his day and generation—the discovery of the Americas.

The reputation of Suárez, on the other hand, does not depend upon his treatment of any single concrete situation of his own day or of any other day. His statement of law and its philosophy was in such terms as to apply equally to his day or to any other day.

Through the discussion of a concrete situation, Victoria formulated the principles of the modern law of nations and pointed the way to their philosophic conception; through the discussion of theoretical positions, Suárez developed, we may say, a philosophy of law applicable to concrete situations. From a different approach, they reached a common goal—the establishment of a single and universal standard of right and wrong in the relations of individuals within a state, in the relations of states with one another and in the relations of the international community composed of these individuals and of these states.

* * *

Now Suárez has given us three masterpieces dealing with law, as such, with its different branches and with the fundamental principles inherent in each. The first of these masterpieces, the one with which we are immediately concerned, is the *Tractatus de Legibus ac Deo Legislatore*, a large volume of twenty books, published at Coimbra in the year 1612, Suárez being then *prima* professor of theology at the University of Coimbra and its crowning glory, as Victoria had been previously at Salamanca; the second, the *Defensio Fidei Catholicae adversus Anglicanae Sectae Errores*, published in

1613, also at Coimbra, the occasion for which was the oath of allegiance which James I of England and VI of Scotland had exacted from his Catholic subjects, unjustly in their opinion, in the opinion of their Church and, we may add, in the opinion of posterity; and the third of the philosophical trinity was the *Opus de Triplici Virtute Theologica*, left in manuscript at his death in 1617 and published four years later simultaneously at Coimbra and Lyons.

It may seem strange to the uninitiated that the portion of the latter work dealing with Charity is devoted to war, but this was entirely proper according to the theology of his Church, which considered it to be an act of charity to reclaim the erring from the evil of their international ways by an act of force, if such were necessary. In this connection, it may be said in passing that the treatment of war by Suárez is, to all intents and purposes, similar to, though not identical with, that of Victoria, thus demonstrating beyond peradventure that, whether implicit or express, the philosophy of each, at least in the matter of war, was both in essence and in application the same.

* * *

For present purposes we need only examine certain portions of the vast treatise *De Legibus*—those dealing with the specific phases and classifications of law, their differences, and therefore their different applications. Let us begin as Suárez begins, with the origin and authority of all law, and first with the *Proemium*, or, in the language of the present day, the Introduction.[1]

Law is of God, whether derived directly or through a human legislator, and, this being the case, "the authority for all laws must ultimately be ascribed to Him."

To turn for a moment to the third book, "What are the elements of law?" They are three in number: the first, "its binding force with respect to the conscience," which Suárez called "its directive force"; the second, "its coercive force," by virtue whereof a violation of the law is punishable; and lastly, "the force by which a definite form is laid down for contracts and similar legal acts," so that an act contrary to the prescribed form is invalid.

Now law has a twofold nature. It is *lex* or *jus*. Of each of these in turn.

Law in the sense of *lex* Suárez first defines in the terms of St. Thomas, for, although St. Thomas was a Dominican and the great glory of that order, he was adopted as its own by every order of the Catholic Church; and at the present day, by the Encyclical of Pope Leo XIII, under date of August 4,

---

[1] The quotations from Suárez dealt with in the present volume are from a provisional English translation, in manuscript, of the Latin text of selections from his *De Legibus ac Deo Legislatore*, which translation, revised where necessary, will appear, together with translations of selections from the *Defensio Fidei* and of the complete text of Disputations XIII and XVIII from the *De Triplici Virtute Theologica*, in a volume of the Classics of International Law in the near future, accompanied by a photographic reproduction of the Latin texts in a separate volume of the series.   It is therefore impossible to give for the quotations footnote citations to the English translation, and it seems undesirable to give references to the original editions of the Latin texts—from which the translations are made—as such texts are not only difficult to read, but difficult of access.

1879, and a brief of exactly a year later, the doctrine of St. Thomas is declared to be the doctrine of the Catholic Church.[1]

Now this St. Thomas as a youngster was "a dumb ox" to his fellow students. However, to his master, Albertus Magnus—now a saint of the Church—he was even then a youth with a marvelous future. "You call him a Dumb Ox," he cried: "I tell you this Dumb Ox shall bellow so loud that his bellowings will fill the world." [2]

What, then, is law in the definition of St. Thomas? "Law," he said, "is a species of rule and measure in accordance with which one is induced to act or is restrained from acting." This is, however, only a point of departure for Suárez. The definition seemed, for his purposes, to be "too broad and general," for, without modification or explanation, law so defined would apply not only to human beings—generously defined by Suárez as "rational creatures"—but also to other creatures, said by human beings to be less rational. Again—for Suárez had one of the keenest minds of the Jesuit order, noted for keenness and for discrimination—the definition of St. Thomas was, in his opinion, too broad and too general, because, taken without modification or explanation, it "would relate not only to moral

---

[1] "Now above all the Doctors of the Schools towers the figure of Thomas Aquinas, the leader and master of them all, who, as Cajetan observes, 'because he had the utmost reverence for the Doctors of antiquity, seems to have inherited in a way the intellect of all.' [On II. ii, qu. 148, art. 4, in finem]."—Leo XIII, Encyclical *Aeterni Patris*, August 4, 1879; in *Acta Sanctae Sedis* (Rome 1879), Vol. XII, p. 97 *et seq.*

"We, for the glory of Almighty God and the honour of the Angelic Doctor, for the increase of the sciences, and for the common benefit of human society, declare by Our Supreme Authority, that St. Thomas Aquinas is Patron of Studies in Universities, Colleges, Lyceums, Catholic Schools; and We desire that he be so held by all. . . ."—Leo XIII, Brief of August 4, 1880; *ibid.*, Vol. XIII, p. 56 *et seq.*

The views of Pope Leo XIII were confirmed by his distinguished successors:

". . . the capital theses in the philosophy of St. Thomas are not to be placed in the category of opinions capable of being debated one way or another, but are to be considered as the foundations upon which the whole science of natural and divine things is based. . . ." Pius X, *Motu Proprio "Doctoris Angelici,"* June 29, 1914; in *Acta Apostolicae Sedis, commentarium officiale Annus VI* (1914), Vol. VI, p. 336 *et seq.*

"We are happy to recall that the philosophy of Aquinas was revived by the authority and at the instance of Leo XIII; the merit of Our Illustrious Predecessor in so doing is such, as we have said elsewhere, that if he had not been the author of many acts and decrees of surpassing wisdom, this alone would be sufficient to establish his undying glory. Pope Pius X of saintly memory followed shortly afterwards in his footsteps, more particularly in his *Motu Proprio 'Doctoris Angelici.'* . . .

"Let everyone therefore inviolably observe the prescription contained in the Codex of Canon Law that 'the study of philosophy and theology and the teaching of these sciences to their students must be accurately carried out by professors [in seminaries, etc.] according to the arguments, doctrine and principles of St. Thomas which they are inviolately to hold'; and may they conform to this rule so faithfully as to be able to describe him in very truth as their master."—Pius XI, Encyclical *Studiorum Ducem*, June 29, 1923, *ibid.*, *Annus XV*, Vol. XV, p. 309 *et seq.*

The provisions of the canons mentioned above are as follows:

"*Canon* 589: Religious who have already studied their humanities should devote themselves for two years at least to philosophy and for four years to theology, following the teaching of St. Thomas (cf. *canon* 1366 § 2) in accordance with the instructions of the Holy See."

"*Canon* 1366 § 2: The study of philosophy and theology and the teaching of these sciences to their students must be accurately carried out by professors [in seminaries, etc.] according to the arguments, doctrine, and principles of St. Thomas which they are inviolately to hold."—*Codex Iuris Canonici, Pii X Pont. Max. iussu digestus, Benedicti Papae XV auctoritate promulgatus* (Rome, 1917). *Canon* 589, p. 170; *Canon* 1366 § 2, p. 398.

[2] G. K. Chesterton, *St. Thomas Aquinas* (New York, 1933), p. 74.

matters, but also to artificial matters, not only to the good and upright, but also to the base." Suárez, however, found a final and a grave "obstacle," as far as his purpose was concerned, to the acceptance of this definition, for, he said, "it would follow that counsels are to be included under law," whereas his opinion was that "according to the faith, counsels are clearly distinct from precepts," from which he draws the conclusion that "they are not included under 'law,' strictly speaking."

What, then, was Suárez' conception of law? "That which pertains to customary conduct [*mores*]," by which definition Suárez contracted, as it were, "the description given by St. Thomas, so that it runs as follows: law is a measure, so to speak, of moral acts". For, although law may otherwise meet the three requirements, absence of the moral element, we add in our own behalf, from any and every definition of law as applicable to human beings, is fatal.

What, then, in a word, is the definition of law according to the moral system of Suárez? We do not need to speculate. He gives it squarely and distinctly within the compass of a single sentence—"strictly and absolutely speaking, only that which is a measure of rectitude, viewed absolutely, and consequently, only that which is a right and virtuous rule, can be called law." With the humility becoming a commentator, may we not express the hope that one day this definition may find its place not only in every municipal statute, but in the law of nations?

So much at present for law as a rule of action.

But what of *jus*, in which the moral element not only enters but predominates? *Jus*, strictly speaking, Suárez defines as "a certain moral faculty which every man has, either over his own property or with respect to that which is due him." Illustrations? "The owner of a thing is said to have a right"—that is *jus*—Suárez continues, "in that thing, and the laborer is said"—to give the second illustration by which Suárez drives home his definition—"to have that right to his wages by reason of which he is declared worthy of his hire." For this phase of the subject he had even higher authority than that of St. Thomas, which authority Suárez himself intimates.

What, then, is the distinction between *lex* and *jus*? *Lex* may justify possession; but *jus* is not merely a matter of law—it is the right itself. Where *lex* is appropriate, *jus* is also appropriate; but *jus* has a further implication. From the etymological standpoint, *jus* and *lex*, if not synonymous, have necessarily a point in common. "*Jus*," Suárez informs us, is derived "from *jubendum*" and "*lex* rests on ordering (*jussio*), or command." The consequence? It is that, so far as an order or a command is concerned, the two may seem to be synonymous, but, in the language of Suárez, "the word *jus* has come to possess certain other connotations which have not been transferred to the term *lex*." Of this he gives a number of illustrations. "The act of a judge is thus wont to be designated by the term *jus*." What are

the reasons?   "Because it ought to be performed in accordance with the laws
(*leges*), or because it sometimes seems to establish a law (*lex*), . . .; so that
the judge, when he exercises his office, is said to declare the law (*jus dicere*)."

The outstanding theologians were, it would seem, as much at home with
the Roman law as with the law of their Church; indeed, both were of Latin
origin.   But perhaps it is well, thus early in the discussion of Suárez' conception of law in its various phases and aspects, to show the nature and the
extent of this familiarity.

Where does he find this function of the judge in relation to law?   In a
"title of the *Digest*:[1] 'If any one fails to obey him who declares the law.'"
In behalf of the law of his Church, Suárez adds: "Moreover, in the canon
law [2] we find the words: 'Outside of his own territory, he who declares the
law may be disobeyed with impunity'"—a statement which we shall see is
fundamental with Suárez, when he treats of domicile.

But if *jus* is to be taken as a command, to the extent that it is synonymous
with *lex*, it has nevertheless an ethical implication, whereas *lex* has a merely
physical or material content—a distinction pointed out by St. Thomas, who
appears to have had in mind the Roman law and who, according to Suárez,
says that "even the art itself by which one determines what is just, is sometimes called *jus*."[3]   To enforce this distinction, Suárez himself appeals to
the Roman law,[4] "in which Ulpian quotes with approval the definition of
Celsus" to the effect that "*jus* is the art of the good and the equitable."
Whereupon Suárez comments that "this definition would be suited, not so
much to law (*lex*) itself, as to jurisprudence (*juris prudentiae*)," adding:
"unless 'art' is taken in a broad sense, as referring to any method or measure
of operation."

What, then, is the conclusion of Suárez on this phase of the question?
"Through usage," he says, "the term *lex* is properly applied both to written
and to non-written law, so that *jus* in so far as it refers to *lex* is used inter-
changeably with that term, and the two words are considered as synonyms."
However, this does not mean that the two terms are wholly synonymous.
They are only the same as far as they go together; but *jus* advances from the
material domain of "command" to enter that of "justice," as distinguished
from *lex*.

Is there then a distinction between *jus* and "the equitable and the
good?"—a question which arises if we consider, as Suárez does, that "*jus*
is precisely the same as that which is just, while the latter"—meaning that
which is just—"is, in turn, precisely the equitable and the good."   Let us
first examine the meaning of "equity".   According to Suárez, "in one
sense, it stands for natural equity", which, in his opinion, "is identical with
natural justice."   In Aristotle's conception, it is "the emendation of that
which is [legally] just"; but it is rather, in the words of Suárez, "the source

---

[1] *Digest*, II, iii.   [2] *Sext*, I. ii. 2.
[3] *Summa*, II. ii., qu. 57, art. 1, ad 1.   [4] *Digest*, I. i. 1, § 1.

or rule thereof." The Latin term *"aequitas"* may be taken, however, "in another sense . . . as being a prudent moderation of the written law *(lex),"* that is, it transcends "the exact, literal interpretation" of the written statute. "In this sense," Suárez continues, *"aequitas* is spoken of . . . as being opposed to *jus* in its strict meaning." This, it may be said in passing, is the modern conception of equity.

Considering equity in this sense, Suárez holds that "the terms 'equitable' *(aequum)* and 'good' *(bonum)* are applied . . . to that which does indeed of itself possess these qualities, even though it may appear to be at variance with the letter of the law *(lex)."* Stated in another way, the judge may temper his application of the law by a judgment *ex aequo et bono*, on the basis of right reason and justice, putting into effect that ancient maxim of equity: "The letter killeth but the spirit maketh alive."

In a few phrases Suárez now states the whole philosophy of equity: "In the interpretation of the laws, the good and the equitable should always be regarded; even if it be needful at times to temper the rigor of the words, in order not to depart from what is naturally equitable and good."

With this as a background, Suárez comes to close quarters with *"jus,"* saying that he will use it "in its second and proper connotation," so that the term "will become synonymous with *lex* but only in so far as we shall now be speaking of *lex*, too, in a general manner."

What, then, is law? To this question which we put Suárez himself replies that it "is a kind of rule, establishing or pointing out, in regard to its own subject matter or the operation with which it is concerned that mean which is to be preserved for the sake of right and fitting action." Here we have *jus* in disguise, that is to say, implied, without express mention, but nevertheless completely permeating the definition. It is a universal rule having, as Suárez says, "relation to all persons, in due proportion." And summing it all up, he gives his definition in a single, brief, and weighty sentence: "Law is a common, just, and stable precept, sufficiently promulgated." It is common in that it applies to all; it is just in that it is equitable and moral; it is a precept, meaning a rule of action; it is stable, because of its permanent nature; and above and beyond all, it is not something secret, for it must be made known and in such a way that, to paraphrase another ancient maxim, ignorance of it will be no excuse.

It will already be evident that we are dealing with the subject of law as treated by one who, although he was not a member of the legal profession in the strict sense of the term, was nevertheless, in the theory of law, a jurist to his fingertips.

* * *

The second of the books of *De Legibus* is for us Suárez' *magnum opus*, dealing as it does with the eternal law, the natural law and the *jus gentium*, in the consideration of which he assumes his rightful place as the founder of the philosophy of law in its various phases, including the law of nations.

For this reason, our task will be a somewhat close analysis of the second book, and, without ceasing to be an analysis, it will rely upon and reproduce in no small measure the very language of Suárez.

Let us begin with the "eternal law," for the reason that it rightly occupies the "first place" with Suárez, "on account of its dignity and excellence," and for the further reason, which must be stated in his very words—because it is his fundamental conception, without which his system would not be, indeed could not be, what it is—that "it is the source and origin of all laws."

Next of the "natural law" and of the link between the two. "Natural law," he says, "is the first system whereby the eternal law has been applied or made known to us," and this law of nature, as it is often called, "is made known to us," Suárez continues, "in a twofold way, first through natural reason, and secondly through the law of the Decalogue written on the Mosaic tablets."

And the "law of nations," for which Suárez uses the term "*jus gentium*," the only term by which it was known in his day, "is of all systems the most closely related to the natural law."

These categories and their inter-relations are appropriately set forth by Suárez by way of the introduction to the second book.

In the third chapter, Suárez develops his idea of the eternal law, saying that it "is a free decree of the Will of God, Who lays down the order to be observed either generally, by [the separate] parts of the universe with respect to the common good or else specifically, by intellectual creatures in their free actions." Here we have what may be called its human application.

The eternal law may be looked at from two points of view. In the first place, being eternal, it is "independent of external promulgation," and in this sense it is without "relation to creatures existing for the moment." It is, in short, apart from all things created. It is the source as well as the law; it is timeless and ageless. It is, in other words, the first cause.

From the second point of view, this eternal law is "promulgated and binding at the same time," and it may be called "divine" in so far as it has a "temporal relation to creatures existing at the time," the term "divine" connoting "adequate external communication and promulgation." The promulgation, Suárez adds, may not be necessary to divine law, but for human knowledge of it there must be "some revealing token or sign whereby it is adequately promulgated," and, being thus promulgated, it is a divine and visible law and the means of application of the eternal law to the affairs of men.

The divine law being related to or a part of the eternal law and revealed from time to time, its binding force "proceeds," Suárez says," immediately from" the eternal. And since it is applicable to human beings, it may be called "human law"—but only in its application, not in its nature. Now there is a human law which is not divine, in that it is made by human beings

and, derived from that source, its binding force is not divine; for the human law is not eternal but "something created and temporal, inasmuch as this law is formed and perfected in the mind and will of man," and therefore is "a law of man and not of God Himself." Nevertheless, "human law is an effect of eternal law," since it is only law "by reason of its participation" in the eternal; in other words, human law, to be law, must be in accord with the eternal verities, or, as we have previously said, the first cause; or, in the Greek conception, it must conform to what they were pleased to call "design in nature."

Human law has, nevertheless, its own binding force, to the extent that "it is dependent upon principles of the eternal law." And the example is: "the precept that obedience is due to superiors." Human law, however, is to be righteous, that is to say, it is to be just and it is to be moral. Therefore it should, in Suárez' language, "conform to the eternal," from which it follows that the human law is related to the eternal law, although not in the same direct sense as is the divine law, which may be defined as the eternal law made evident. Now the immediate source of the divine law is the eternal law, without the intervention of a human agency, while the human law is not only administered, but is formulated by men, "the latter," in Suárez' language, "being not only an incidental cause . . . that is, not merely establishers and appliers of this law; but also the essential cause— that is, the creators of the law itself." What is the result? The force and efficacy of the human law comes "directly from the will of the human legislator." And Suárez sets forth in two sentences, which deserve to be called "classic," the obligation of the divine and human law:

1. In the case of the divine law, the obligation is derived immediately from God Himself, since in so far as that law exists in man, it has no binding force save as it manifests the divine reason, or will.

2. In human law, however, the obligation is not derived immediately from God; for in so far as human law exists in those who are subject thereto, it has an immediate relation to the will of the prince who has the power to create a new law, as distinct from the divine law, and from his will the obligation directly emanates, although fundamentally this obligation proceeds in its entirety from the eternal law.

But the difference is more apparent than real, as is also stated in classic terms by Suárez:

All men necessarily behold within themselves some sort of participation in the eternal law, since there is no rational person who does not in some manner judge that the honorable course of action must be followed and the base avoided; and in this sense, it is said that men have some knowledge of the eternal law.

It may be asked, according to the conception of Suárez, and indeed of Christendom, is not man the handiwork of God? And what could be more natural than that he should be, at least in some degree, a reflection of his Creator? But it is not given—to paraphrase Suárez—to every man to see the divine both in and through the human law.

We now pass with Suárez to the second division, "natural law," which he defines in a preliminary way as consisting "in a true judicial act of the mind." This brief definition, however, he feels should be expanded. The natural law is not evident as are the ground beneath us and the heavens above us; for the natural law may be called, he immediately says, "the natural light of the intellect, inherently adapted for prescribing what must be done . . . since men retain that law in their hearts, although they may be engaged in no [specific] act of reflection or judgment." The discovery of the natural law may be by means of deliberate reflection, but it may also be instinctive; in either case it is, as Suárez says, the result of "the natural light of the intellect." It is a thing inherent in man, in that it is in the hearts of men because written there by God Himself—on the authority of St. Paul—and, for us of the United States, on the lesser authority of Alexander Hamilton. For does not Hamilton say, in his reply to the "Westchester Farmer," that human rights "are not to be rummaged for among old parchments or musty records. They are written, as with a sunbeam, in the whole volume of human nature, by the hand of the divinity itself, and can never be erased or obscured by mortal power." [1]

Natural law, as we have said, is inherent. So also is conscience. "Nevertheless," says Suárez, "the two are different. For the term 'law' has reference to a rule respecting those things which should be done and framed in general terms; whereas conscience is a practical dictate in a particular case, so that it is the application of the law to a particular act, so to speak, rather than the law itself." Natural law is the general standard; conscience is the standard of the individual.

Let us state in a single sentence the obligation of the natural law. As an emanation of the eternal law, the law natural carries with it an obligation proceeding from the divine will, that "men shall be bound to obey that which right reason dictates."

Now what of human law, which, for present purposes, is of two kinds? Both are human law in the sense that they are not divine. The first is custom or the common law. This kind of law is not made by a particular person but grows by human action. The human law considered in this general sense carries with it its own obligation, and this obligation, as will appear later, flows from the natural law itself, and has an inherent sanction. Secondly, there is human law in the specific sense, that is, the law of the legislature, or, as we would say, the statute. This law creates an obligation and therefore should have a sanction; but the obligation, like the statute, is man-made; and depending upon human will, it must be express, in order that the obligation may be enforceable.

There is, however, a further distinction going to the very essence of things. A statute makes a thing a crime and therefore fixes a punishment for its

[1] *The Works of Alexander Hamilton*, edited by Henry Cabot Lodge (New York, 1903), I, p. 113.

violation.   A statute makes wrong the act which it condemns (whereas in the domain of the natural law, a thing is in essence good or bad); and a natural law does not make bad what it condemns but prohibits it because it is bad, in other words, because it is inherently evil.   In this sense the natural law partakes of, and indeed is, divine law.   What is the result?   The natural law is a moral law and therefore "embraces all precepts or moral principles which are plainly characterized by the righteousness necessary to virtuous conduct." The converse is also true, in that the natural law prohibits things essentially evil.   From the statement of Suárez there are two immediate and inevitable conclusions, the first of which states and defines the way in which the law of nature is revealed.   It is made evident, as we would expect from what Suárez has already said, by "natural illumination," and the consequence is that "the natural law is binding in conscience," for the judge in the forum of conscience is natural reason itself.

Now it is a truism among writers on international law that the law of nature is immutable.   But Suárez was not content with truisms.   The natural law being synonymous with rational nature, it "cannot of itself lapse or suffer change" but will, as Suárez says, endure as long as the human being is possessed of reason and freedom of will.   Natural law, therefore, exists and it continues to exist; but it applies to conditions which are not immutable.   The precept is unchangeable; its application may vary from age to age.   For in Suárez' own language, "the natural law discerns the mutability contained in the subject matter itself," from which it follows that the mutability existing in the nature of things is, as it were, a constant factor and, again to quote Suárez, the natural law "adapts its own precepts to this mutability, prescribing . . . a certain sort of conduct for one condition, and another sort of conduct for another condition," so that Suárez is justified in logically drawing the conclusion from his premises that "the law in itself remains at all times unchanged, although according to our manner of speaking and by an extrinsic process of metonymy, it would *seem*"—we emphasize the word—"after a fashion, to undergo change."

There are certain positive commands of natural law, and there are certain things which are permitted, conceded or allowed, or, in the language of Suárez, things "permissive, negative, or concessive."   With the things prescribed we have already dealt, an example being those things which are prohibited by the natural law as being inherently evil or commanded by it as being intrinsically good and "necessary to virtuous conduct."   In the second group which partakes of the nature of a permission and not a command—"there fall many things which . . . are permissible, or conceded, to men."   What are these things?   "A community of goods, human liberty and the like."   And here Suárez proceeds to state how such things, being merely permissible, may change without violating the law of nature.   For example, he instances changes which are "in accordance with the demands of reason."   "Nakedness is natural to man," according to Suárez.   This

nakedness, however, does not "require covering in the state of innocence; whereas, in the fallen condition of human nature, natural reason imposes a different requirement. So also liberty is natural to man." Why? "Since he possesses it by the force of natural law; yet the law of nature does not forbid the loss of his liberty." We may ourselves advance an example: a captive might under the ancient conception be put to death, or if his life were spared he might be deprived of his liberty; and neither would have been contrary to the law of nature. Such is a first group of things permissible.

There is a second dealing with another phase of the subject—the "foundation" of a right not absolutely prescribed by natural law, the foundation being "in a natural disposition." This is the case of a son inheriting from an intestate father, according to the *Digest*.[1] The example given is of so frequent occurrence that it may not seem to need comment; yet, as Suárez uses it in order to establish a fundamental principle of large implication, he should be heard in its behalf and in his own words: "For the natural law, although it does not absolutely prescribe that this shall be so, does incline toward this arrangement, which follows from it naturally, so to speak, unless an impediment arises from some other source." In like manner, he instances by way of example the credence given to two witnesses. Proof being needed, two witnesses are considered sufficient for the requirements, and this custom, according to Suárez, may be said "to pertain to the natural law," in its permissive rather than in its prescriptive phase, "unless," he adds, "for special causes some other [requirement] is added, or imposed [in substitution]." Here the Bible may be quoted in his behalf; for is it not said: "In the mouth of two or three witnesses every word may stand"?[2]

Suárez now takes up certain "precepts of natural law, . . . dealing with pacts, agreements, or obligations." The first two are truly "introduced through the will of men," and the obligations he has in mind are also those created by the human will. The examples he gives are laws for the "observance of vows, . . . whether these be made in simple form or confirmed by oath." They form a special class. But the principle involved applies to all contracts and also the rights to which they give rise.

Such are, it is believed, the stock examples of natural rights; the duties and obligations of which are stated in three simple Latin words, *Pacta sunt servanda*. With this natural precept of three words, law and order and fair dealing are possible; without it, unfair dealing, leading, it may be, to anarchy. It is the foundation of a governed world; for, if solemn agreements are not to be kept, there is no such thing as law and order, natural or human. Indeed there are many jurists—among them international lawyers of repute —who regard these three words as stating the whole obligation of the law natural with all of the proper and reasonable consequences which flow from such obligation. Even the positivists accept the phrase, unconscious, it

[1] XXXVIII. vi. 7, at end.   [2] St. Matthew, xviii, 16.

may be, that in so doing they are stamping with their approval the obligation of natural law and its necessary or reasonable consequences; in other words, by admitting the obligation of natural law they recognize, perhaps unwittingly, the existence of a natural jurisprudence.

In order that there be no doubt about the matter and its importance, it may be said that there is a consensus of opinion in the civilized world that, if the common rights of men are not natural rights, they are, even if "acquired," so fundamental as to be beyond the power of prince, legislature, or even the people themselves to suppress.

So much for precepts of the natural law—or at least their consequences—in which the hand of man is visible.   There are others equally binding, as Suárez says, because of their "subject-matter, and independently of any prior consent by human will."   These are affirmative—"positive precepts of religious devotion to God, of filial piety, of mercy, and of almsgiving to one's neighbor"—and negative, of which examples are those "against killing, against slander, and similar prohibitions."   In so far as the precepts introduced by the will of man are influenced by human will, they are mutable to that extent, whereas the precepts independent of human will are, as Suárez himself says, "immutable."   The latter precepts are concerned with timeless truths, the former with "the human power of free-will", which is itself "exceedingly changeable," and frequently requires "correction and alteration."   This simple statement of Suárez is of immense importance, as it recognizes the change in law from time to time, to meet the changing conditions upon which the progress and the civilization of the world depend; in other words, we have a rigid law as regards the fundamentals of right and wrong but a variable law in their application to changing human conditions.

It follows as a necessary consequence from the immutability of the natural law as such that "no human power, even though it be the Papal power"—it is to be borne in mind that Suárez is speaking—"can abrogate any proper precept of natural law, nor truly and essentially restrict such a precept, nor grant a dispensation from it."

He advances four proofs in behalf of this positive assertion.   As Suárez is considered the last of the schoolmen—meaning the last who had something worth saying and said it in the manner of the schoolmen—the proofs in behalf of the assertion under consideration are given in his own words as a perfect example of his mastery of the scholastic method.

1. The first proof of this assertion is drawn from the statements made in the preceding chapter; for it has been shown [in that chapter] that the natural law, in so far as its precepts are concerned, is by its very nature unchangeable; and men cannot change that which is unchangeable; therefore, . . .

This proof is confirmed in the true scholastic manner "by the fact that the natural law, in all its precepts, relates to the natural qualities of mankind; and man cannot change the nature of things; therefore, ..."

Suárez now passes to the second proof, in which the assertion in question is proved by the fact that

2. In the case of every precept of natural law, God is the law-giver; and man cannot change a law that God has established, since an inferior cannot prevail as against his superior.

The next proof is the argument that

3. The natural law is the foundation of human law, therefore, human law cannot derogate from natural law; [since], otherwise, it would destroy its own foundation, and, consequently, itself.

These three proofs would seem to be unanswerable; but Suárez, being a schoolman, is not content to convince; his purpose is to overwhelm his adversary. Therefore he continues:

4. If human law could derogate from natural law, it would be possible for the former to make an enactment in opposition to the latter, since one can conceive of no other way of changing natural law; but human law cannot make such an enactment; therefore, . . .

To readers of his day, this method of argument would seem the natural way of proceeding, but having pity, as it were, on us moderns, who have fallen into strange ways, Suárez, after having proved his major premise, calls our attention specifically to the minor premise, and incidentally clinches his argument beyond all peradventure of dispute. "The minor premise is proved thus: what is contrary to natural law is intrinsically evil; therefore the human law in question would relate to an intrinsically evil matter, and in consequence would not [truly] constitute either *jus* or *lex*." This would indeed be unfortunate; for if it is neither, it is nothing in the realm of law.

But still Suárez is not content. For his proof of the minor premise, he must have a confirmation and he finds it in "the fact that, for this same reason, a custom"—mark the word—"opposed to natural law cannot make a legal rule." Hitherto he has been relying upon the syllogism, its parts and its consequences, but in order to make assurance doubly or trebly sure, he invokes the authority of the *Decretals* [1] and "the Gloss thereon," to the effect that "the natural law is immutable in so far as concerns its commands and prohibitions." To us this would seem sufficient, but Suárez must have another authority, and he finds it in a similar passage "in the Gloss on *Decretum*, I. v. 1, where Gratian"—himself the compiler of the *Decretum*— "says that the natural law is unchangeable; a statement which he repeats in . . . *Decretum*, I. vi, last canon."

There is, however, a second brand of precepts of natural law which constitutes an exception to the assertion which Suárez has so convincingly proved. For there are, as he has already informed us, certain precepts of the natural law depending for their binding force "upon a prior consent of human will" and upon its efficacy "to issue in some action." This kind of precept "may sometimes be subjected to human dispensation." Why? Because such a dispensation does not involve "a direct and absolute aboli-

[1] I. iv. 11.

tion of the obligation of natural law" but merely a remission, which affects the subject-matter of the precept.   The remission which brings about the change "is not contrary to natural law," because it depends not upon a change of the law itself but upon a change in human volition.   This being the case, a superior may, in this sense, alter the obligation of the natural law, but only in remitting its obligation in the special manner thus indicated by Suárez.   The essence of the transaction is the remission of a duty or an obligation.   Such remission may be, and usually is, by a superior to whom the duty or obligation is due.   On the other hand, the private individual may, in certain instances, take such action of his own volition, as in the case of one who remits "the natural obligation arising from a promise," or the "obligation arising from a mutual contract by effecting a donation": in plain English, the remission of a debt or indebtedness.   In this case, the law upon which the obligation depends still remains, but the subject-matter having changed hands, the obligation ceases.   The "dispensation," to use the technical expression, is, as Suárez rightly says, "from fact rather than from law."

But the change in subject-matter may be brought about by laws as well as by individuals, superior or private.   The example of this which Suárez gives is derived from human law, and he here instances the "*jus gentium* or the civil law*," that is to say, the law of nations—or the municipal law of a single nation.   Through either of these there may be "effected in the subject-matter of the natural law a change of such sort that, by reason of it, the obligation imposed by natural law will also change."

Let us take an example—not merely a change, but a succession of changes in the subject-matter brought about by the *jus gentium*.   There is the precept, "Thou shalt not kill"—a natural precept, if ever there was one. The precept presupposes that there is no just cause for taking life.   But suppose a war breaks out—to use the most common example in antiquity and one which is not wholly a stranger to our own day.   A life for a life: he who would kill may himself be killed, even after capture.   This was both recognized and regularized by the *jus gentium*—the change making that legal which otherwise would not have been so under the natural law.   This, however, is but the first change.   Later the procedure was not to put prisoners to death but to retain them as captives, depriving them permanently of their natural right to liberty, that procedure being more serviceable, inasmuch as a living slave was more profitable than a dead enemy.   This, too, was recognized and approved by the law of nations.   Still later, the prisoner was allowed— or others in his behalf—to purchase freedom from slavery (or some other form of captivity) by the payment of a round sum technically known as "ransom money."   Again the change of subject-matter entered into the law of nations.   Finally, prisoners are today exchanged for prisoners, as it is apparently to the advantage of each of the contending parties to get rid of what might at times be an incumbrance, and to have returned to them the

one-time prisoners. However, the element of profit is not overlooked. Private soldiers are exchanged for private soldiers and officers for officers— but only officers of the same rank. Here we have an example, or rather a series of examples, running through countless ages, bearing out the truth of Suárez' statement.

As to the basis in reason of changes of whatsoever kind which may affect the obligation of the natural law without changing the nature of the law, we must assuredly quote the exact language of Suárez, generalizing the question as it does and adding an interesting and a priceless illustration taken from the first authority in the Church after St. Paul, and one to whom international law is forever indebted. "And finally, the rational basis of the assertion in question is that such a mode of change is not inconsistent with the necessary and changeless character of the natural law; and that, for the rest, it is convenient and frequently necessary for men, in accordance with the various changes of estate which befall them." Suárez now invokes the spiritual authority of St. Augustine in the form of a material illustration: "In this connection, too, one may fittingly apply the familiar illustration drawn from Augustine, that just as the science of medicine lays down certain precepts for the sick, and others for the well, certain ones for the strong, and others for the weak, although the rules of medicine do not therefore undergo essential change, but merely become multiple in their number, so that some serve on one occasion, and others, on another occasion; even so, the natural law, while it remains [in itself] the same, lays down one precept for one occasion, another, for another occasion; and is binding [in one of its rules] at one time, and not binding previously and subsequently, and this without undergoing any change in itself [but merely] because of a change in the subject-matter."

There is precept of the natural law with which we of the United States have had a long and painful but a chastening experience: liberty for the white; slavery for the black; liberty, now, fortunately, for all human beings. Of "liberty" Suárez says: "Liberty, rather than slavery, is [a precept] of the natural law." The reason? That "nature has made men free in a positive sense, so to speak, with an intrinsic right to liberty, whereas it has not made them slaves in this positive sense, properly speaking." The American Declaration of Independence set forth the same principle in recognizing that "all men are created equal," with a right to "life, liberty and the pursuit of happiness." Now, liberty, in the conception of Suárez, was a natural right —indeed, a precept of the law of nature. Nevertheless, it was a right, Suárez says, which man might renounce, and in the case of punishment, society might renounce it in his behalf. In that sense, therefore, slavery or a form of servitude is permissible by the law of nature. Today, fortunately, we no longer avail ourselves of this permission as regards slavery, and indeed the individual can not, of his own free will, make himself a slave. He can only be deprived of his liberty by due process of law, as Suárez later implies,

and then solely as a means of punishment, or for the good of society, as in the case of insane persons.

"Nature," Suárez continues in the same passage, "has conferred upon men in common dominion over all things, and consequently has given to every man a power to use these things." "But nature," according to Suárez and according to writers generally, does not confer "private property rights," to be exercised by individuals to the exclusion of the other members of the community. Nevertheless, ownership of private property is today the rule. Community of property, to be sure, existed under natural law; but was it prescribed by natural law? It may or may not have been so prescribed, in the opinion of Suárez, but while common ownership continued, there was, in his language, "a positive precept of natural law, to the effect that no one should be prohibited or prevented from making the necessary use of the common property." This was so in the days before private property; and indeed it is still so, as Suárez points out, "with regard to those things which are common, and for so long as they are not in any way divided."

It would seem that the high seas constitute the best illustration for Suárez' statement that "no one may be prohibited from the common use of such things, generally speaking, that is, aside from cases involving special necessity or a just cause"—such cases, we may add, as necessary jurisdiction over the marginal waters, and occupation of parts of the sea by belligerents in time of war. What is the application of the natural law after division of community into private property has taken place? "The natural law," Suárez says with admirable brevity, "forbids theft, or the undue taking of another's property."

Let us consider somewhat further the matter of liberty, to which Suárez has already referred and upon which we have made an anticipatory comment. "Nature," he says, "although it has granted liberty, and dominion over that liberty, has, nevertheless, not absolutely forbidden that it should be taken away." What are the reasons which justify its withdrawal? Since "man is lord of his own liberty, it is possible for him to sell or alienate the same." Fortunately this disposition of one's self has gone by the board; in other words, we have here an example of a change in the application of the natural law as the result of the civil law, and that subsequent to Suárez.

As could the individual in Suárez' day, so the commonwealth, made up of individuals, could in his day as well as in ours, alienate liberty, "acting through a higher power, which it"—meaning, of course, the commonwealth —"possesses for the government of man." Is this simply because the commonwealth may possess the physical power? No. It must be "for a just cause." What is this cause? "By way of a punishment." And the whole thing is summed up by Suárez in a single sentence: "For nature also gave to man the use and possession of his own life; yet he may sometimes justly be deprived of it, through human agency."

With a firm hand Suárez draws a distinction between mandatory natural

law and the law concerning dominion, whether over self or over property. The former "comprehends rules and principles for right conduct which involve necessary truth, and these," he continues, "are therefore immutable." And the reason is that these rules and principles of the mandatory natural law "are based upon the intrinsic rectitude or perversity of their objects," that is, they command or prohibit a thing because it is good or bad, whereas the civil law—meaning the law applicable within a nation—or the law of the international community makes a thing good or bad by the very fact that it commands or prohibits it.

Thus far of the mandatory natural law.

"The law concerning dominion"—whether over liberty or property—"is merely the subject-matter" of the mandatory law, Suárez meaning thereby that the existence of a certain fact or "a certain condition or habitual state of things," when recognized, is protected by the mandatory natural law.   Thus, as an example, when natural law permitted a change of dominion by the division of community into private property, the mandatory natural law stepped in with the command that private rights should be respected.

The succeeding passage deals with the higher rights, and is quoted without a break, in order to show the manner in which Suárez considers and safeguards such rights, permitting their change under natural law yet protecting the new rights brought into being because of the change.   "It is evident," he proceeds, without a pause, "that all created things, and especially those which are corruptible, are characterized through nature by many conditions that are changeable and capable of being abolished for many causes.   Accordingly, we say of liberty and of any similar lawful right, that even if such a right has been positively granted by nature, it may be changed by human agency, since it is dependent in the individual persons, either upon their own wills, or upon the state, in so far as the latter has lawful power over all private individuals and over their property, to the extent necessary for right government."   This is in essence a philosophy not only of law but of government.

Suárez now passes to a consideration of the two points of view from which natural law may be regarded: the first, natural law, as such; and the second, as it may find its expression in a positive law.   In the latter case, the positive law, in so far as it includes natural law within its terms, is only declaratory, as it can neither make nor unmake the law natural.   It is, in the words of Suárez, "a reminder of the natural law."   It is "declarative," just as were, to use Suárez' illustration, "the moral precepts of the Decalogue in the Old Law."   The same may also be said of those human laws involving natural justice, of which Suárez gives a trio of interesting examples: the first, that a "deposit" is to be returned; the second, that a promise must be "fulfilled"—which would fall under the rubric *Pacta sunt servanda;* and the third, contrary to the unfortunately well-nigh prevailing view of the present day, "that a wife must not be separated from her husband."

Thus in a word the natural law may be declared by the positive law, or it may be considered as it is in itself and, Suárez adds, "as it is conceived or dictated by right reason"—which the learned St. Germaine had said, in his *Doctor and Student*, written and published before Suárez was born, is the English for natural law.

But simple as this may seem when stated by Suárez, he himself felt, as must we who only dabble in the law of nature, that "many natural precepts require a great deal of exposition and interpretation in order that their true sense may be established."

There are various reasons why this should be so.   Among those which Suárez mentions are the fact that "human actions, in so far as concerns their righteous or wicked character, depend to a great extent upon the circumstances and opportunities for their execution."   In English we have a colloquial expression which means much the same thing: "Circumstances alter cases"—the more so as natural law permits the good and prohibits the bad because they are good and bad.   This being the case, we must inquire, Suárez continues, "into the conditions and circumstances under which the act concerned is essentially good or evil," which inquiry—still in the words of Suárez—is "the interpretation of a natural precept with respect to the true sense of that precept."

Now there are two processes which, to a certain extent, are similar and may often be confused.   But Suárez had no intention that either he or his reader should misunderstand the distinction between "equity" and "interpretation"; for, while "interpretation," as distinct from "equity," applies to every law—natural, municipal, or international—ἐπιείκεια (which we shall render as *aequitas*, to avoid the familiar "equity" of chancery in English law) "has no place in any natural precept," as such, "for the law of nature is inherently good and perfect of itself," and a thing perfect can not be perfected by *aequitas*.   More than one authority prior to Suárez had apparently confused "*aequitas*" and "interpretation," and the errors of his predecessors and opponents serve, as it were, to light Suárez on his course.

Take, for example, the precept concerning the "return of a deposit," cited by no less an authority than Cajetan, who appears to have considered such a transaction as a case of "*aequitas*"; but in the opinion of Suárez, what happens is that "we make an interpretation to the effect that it—the precept —is not binding when the return of the deposit would be contrary to justice or to charity."   But this interpretation is not, he informs us, *aequitas*.   In this view of things, there is the clear implication that justice and charity are inherent in the natural law.   In the words of Suárez, "right reason lays down not an absolute dictate that deposits must be returned, but a dictate that they shall be returned only under certain implied conditions required by the principles of justice and charity."   This interpretation does not affect the universal character of the rule of natural law but implies its universality

above and beyond circumstances. In other words, the principle holds; it is the circumstances which change.

Before going further in his discussion of this phase of the question, Suárez considers it well to define ἐπιείκεια—or, as we prefer to say, *aequitas*. It is nothing more nor less than the "emendation of a law, or of that which is legally just." But as natural law is just and is founded upon right reason, which, in turn, is the spokesman of truth, it is clear that natural law cannot be amended. Still dealing with the distinction between "interpretation" and "*aequitas*," Suárez shows at this point the danger of confusion from another source. Supposing that an obligation of the natural law should be held by proper judicial authority to lapse because of a change in the subject-matter—a situation with which Suárez has already dealt—would this be *aequitas?* No, says Suárez, for "this is the result, not of ἐπιείκεια, but of a change in subject-matter." What is the effect of the *aequitas* which Suárez has in mind? It is, in a word, an exemption from the law.

Now this being the case, can there likewise be an exemption from the universal law through interpretation? Suárez answers, as we would expect, in the negative, adding that "a dictate of right reason . . . is imposed universally." This does not mean that with changing conditions it may not lapse under certain circumstances, but it does mean that as long as the circumstances remain unaltered and the law therefore universal, there can be no exemption from it.

As an illustration of the universality which he has in mind, Suárez takes the simplest of examples of philosophical science, the case of a human hand, which science finds should have only five fingers—although not in an absolute sense but in a sufficiently limited sense to permit of exceptions. However, until human hands generally have more or less than five fingers, the finding is universal, that is to say, there can be no change in the application of natural law until the conditions themselves change—in this case, a finger more or less. Under such circumstances, the finding, like natural law would hold and be applicable unless the majority of hands had more or less than five fingers.

It is obvious, therefore, as Suárez proceeds to point out, that in those natural precepts which "are always binding, there is no place for interpretation, since there is no place for variation."

The case is different, however, with reference to precepts which are "not binding for all occasions." The question then arises as to whether the determination of the circumstances under which they are not binding is a matter of *aequitas*. When the natural law in question is expressed in terms of positive human law, then the existence or extent of the obligation may be determined, by both interpretation and *aequitas*, and may even be subject to dispensation. This, however, is a matter of positive law and hence, Suárez says, "has no bearing on the question in hand."

Again, the obligation may be determined "through natural reason itself,"

continues Suárez; but in this case, it is not *aequitas* which is involved, "since there is no exception from the law nor emendation of the precept." There is rather a "simple understanding", which is neither an exception nor an emendation; in other words, an understanding of the law is based not upon *aequitas* but upon the use of reason.

"In the case of positive law" containing a prohibition, to which Suárez now turns, "interpretation by ἐπιείκεια . . . does not refer to the act forbidden by the law; nor to any obscurity in the words of that law," it being here assumed that the "act is one forbidden on the basis of its very form, and that it is comprised within the terms of the law, in their strict sense." On the other hand, the question may arise as to what was the intent of the law-maker, and this is a case when true *aequitas* comes into play. In that event the process should serve to reveal the intention of the lawmaker, for human law is the expression of a human intention, presumed to be just, as otherwise it is not law.

To drive home again his view that *aequitas* has "no place in the natural law," as such, Suárez here definitely and finally separates it from the natural law by the statement that "this procedure, however, has no place in the natural law, because it"—meaning the natural law—"is founded primarily, not upon the will that prohibits, but upon the nature of the inherently evil act itself."

The difference between human and natural law is this: In the human law, we look for the intent of the lawgiver; in natural law, there is no intent—there is a command, a permission, or a prohibition. It may happen that neither the command nor the prohibition is expressly stated, in which case the one or the other is discovered through the application of right reason; but that is a process of understanding, not of seeking the intention of the lawgiver, as is the case with human law.

* * *

Suárez has thus far dealt largely, if not wholly, with natural law, mentioning incidentally the law of the state and the law of that larger community of states, to which law he gives the name of *jus gentium*. Let us for a moment consider the implications of Suárez' conception of the law of nature. In his system natural law is to be looked upon as the foundation upon which he is to erect his structure of justice, national and international. National justice expressed in the form of law and applying to individuals within the state is, as it were, the first story of the structure, upon which international justice, binding alike individuals as such, and individuals grouped in states, can be said to rest. International law, therefore, is based, so to speak, on two firm foundations. But the more fundamental of these foundations is natural law, the law of the human being as such, which he inherits but does not make, for it is the basis of the law of the individuals forming the state, with such additions as may be made by the proper agency of the state from time to time to meet their special needs. These additions measure, as it

were, the extent to which the law of the state is the work of human hands. The *jus gentium*, though not identical with the law of nature, is like it in its generality; for does not Suárez say, speaking of this *jus gentium*, in the opening lines of the seventeenth chapter of Book II, that it has such "a close affinity with the natural law . . . that many persons confuse it therewith, or hold that the *jus gentium* is a part of the natural law; and, furthermore, even in those aspects wherein the two are distinguished, the kinship is very close and the *jus gentium* constitutes an intermediate form, so to speak, between the natural and the human law, a form bordering upon the first of these extremes." But it is also like the non-statutory law of the single state in so far as it is made slowly, and it may be unconsciously, through usage and custom. There is, however, a further element which enters into its making, the agreements of the states—which, in Suárez' lifetime, had not attained the proportions of our day and of our world.

But even though the three forms of law may be distinct, they are one in that the standard of each and all is, or should be, the universal test of right and wrong; and it is the glory of Suárez that to this world, ruled by systems of law—which are in essence, but not in form, the same—he gave an acceptable legal philosophy.

With Suárez the *jus gentium*, which he proposed to analyze, was an existing thing; and that there might be no doubt upon this point in the mind of the reader who happened to thumb the pages of this seventeenth chapter, he proceeds to enumerate the authorities by whom the *jus gentium* was assumed to be "an established fact," as demonstrated by "their very frequent use of the term." What are these authorities? The *Digest* and the *Institutes* of Justinian, the *Decretum* of Gratian, St. Isidore's *Etymologies*, and, in addition, "the Doctors of both canon and civil law," and also St. Thomas and the theologians. In other words, Suárez invokes the consensus of intelligent opinion of the ancient and the mediaeval world in behalf of the existence of a *jus gentium* which had taken moral form in the hands of Victoria, and which was to take a philosophic form in the very tractate of Suárez which we are now discussing.[1]

The law of nations is for Suárez a law in the strict legal sense of the word. But there are, as he has already observed, two kinds of law. There is *lex* on the one hand, and *jus* on the other; and, as *jus* is the concomitant of *"gentium"*—indeed is that upon which *"gentium"* rests—it is essential that Suárez state in even more precise forms the definition of *jus* and the distinctions between its various connotations.

[1] Suárez' words on the question of authorities are so enlightening as to his sources that the reader may prefer to have before his eyes a literal translation of the text: "The existence of the *jus gentium* then, is assumed by all authorities to be an established fact, so we gather, from their very frequent use of the term. For the *jus gentium* is often mentioned in the Civil Law in *Digest*, I. i, 2, and *Institutes*, I. ii, and in the *Decretum*, I, i, and following, from Isidore (*Etymologies*, Bk. V, chap. ii. [V. vi.]); by the Doctors of both Canon and Civil Law, in connection with these and other passages; and by St. Thomas (II. ii, qu. 57, art. 3) and the theologians."

Now this *jus* is, to quote Suárez' exact language, "an equivocal term," and because of that he continues, "its various meanings must be distinguished, that we may employ it only in that acceptation which pertains to our purposes." What are these meanings? The first which Suárez mentions is *jus* in the sense of a "moral faculty over or relating to some thing." Now in this meaning, the faculty in question is a right in the sense that it involves "true dominion or merely a partial dominion," which faculty is, according to St. Thomas, "the true object of justice." "*Jus*" was not only equivocal in Suárez' day; it is such in our own. It is "*recht*" in German, meaning "right" in one sense and "law" in another, and each of the two names in German for the law of nations contains the word *recht* (*völkerrecht* and *internationales recht*). In French, *jus* takes the form of "*droit*," whether it be the *droit des gens* or *droit international*—the exact equivalents of the two German expressions. The same thing may be said of the Italian "*diritto*"—*diritto de gente* and *diritto internazionale*. In Spanish, Suárez' native language, the term is "*derecho*"—*derecho de gentes* and *derecho internacional*. But we must not omit the name by which the law is called in the land of Grotius—*volkenrecht* and *internationaal recht*. In English there is, alas, only the unequivocal "law," whether it be the law of nations or international law, and it may be that the Anglo-Saxon conception of law has lost something of the connection with right which the Romance languages, as well as the Teutonic, preserve—at least in form, if not in substance—through the use of a term which means both right and law.

It is to be observed that in the foreign terminology, in languages other than English, there is at least a moral implication because of the presence of "right," whereas the English term "law" raises no such implication and has in itself no essential connection with right or justice. For the English term is akin not to *jus* but to *lex*[1]—which is but a rule of action without any necessary reference to the moral qualities of right and justice—a fact which may account for the statement we often hear (too often, indeed), that a court is a place where law, not justice, is administered.

But to return to Suárez and his analysis of *jus*. This "*jus*," which may at times mean "right," he now adds "sometimes means law." Law, in the view of Suárez, is "the rule of righteous conduct," and, so conceived, *jus* is that "which establishes a certain equity in things," and therefore this definition constitutes "the rational basis" for accepting *jus* as "law." Upon whose authority? That of St. Thomas himself. For the "rational basis" is synonymous with law, and again the authority is that of St. Thomas. From which it follows, according to Suárez, that we must speak of the first sort of *jus*, that is, the "moral faculty" involving dominion as "practical" (*jus utile*); and the second *jus* as "law," "in relation to righteousness" (*jus honestum*): or, Suárez continues, we may speak "of the first as 'real' (*jus*

---

[1] It seems generally to be conceded that the English "law" is of Teutonic rather than Latin origin, and hence that it is not, as was one time believed, a derivation from *lex*.

reale) and of the second as 'legal' (*jus legale*)." What was the consequence, if not the avowed purpose, of these distinctions? To establish that *jus* in one sense is right in practice or, as Suárez says, right in the "real" sense, and that in the sense of law, it is not right itself but related to righteousness and is primarily legal rather than ethical.

The further consequence of this twofold kind of law in the sense of *jus* is, as Suárez says, its division "into the natural law, the *jus gentium* and the civil law." This three-fold division naturally suggests a definition of the sense in which Suárez is to employ each of the terms. "For the *jus utile*,"— *jus* in practice—he proceeds, "is termed natural when it is granted by or originates within nature." The example of Suárez is "liberty," which "may be said to spring from the natural law." The same *jus utile* appears in a different guise within the state, being civil law. And the example? "The right of prescription." It is now the turn of the *jus gentium*; for the *jus utile* is called the law of nations, "when founded upon the common usage of mankind." As illustrations Suárez cites "the right of passage over public highways, or the right to enslave, introduced by war."

This threefold division of *jus*, which Suárez has been discussing, relates "to the object of justice," as may be inferred, he says, "from a passage in St. Thomas,"—which passage, it may be stated, deals with the relationship between the *jus gentium* and the *jus naturale*.[1]

Now Suárez, although no man had a clearer conception of right and wrong, was primarily engaged in formulating a philosophy for law. Therefore he adds, "we are speaking of the *jus gentium* . . . rather as a species of law." This being the case he turns from the *jus utile* to the second conception of *jus*, that of *jus legale*, which "is also wont to be divided" into natural, civil, and international law.

This conception of law as law we would expect to be confirmed, and in this case, as in many others, it is confirmed by the *Digest* of Justinian.

We here encounter Ulpian's trouble-making definition that "the natural law is shared in common with brute creation, while the *jus gentium* is peculiar to man." The twofold authority, derived in each case from Ulpian, is found in the *Digest*[2] and in the *Institutes*,[3] of which Suárez makes a paraphrase rather than a translation: "The natural law is that which nature teaches to all animate creatures; for it does not pertain exclusively to the human race, but is shared in common with all animate creatures born on land or sea, and to all birds as well."[4] From the point of view of man, it is not agreeable to

---

[1] II. ii. Question 57, art. 3.

[2] *Digest*, I. i. 1, § 3: "*Ius naturale est, quod natura omnia animalia docuit: nam ius istud non humani generis proprium, sed omnium animalium, quae in terra, quae in mari nascuntur avium quoque commune est.*"

[3] *Institutes*, I, ii: "*Ius naturale est, quod natura omnia animalia docuit: nam ius istud non humani generis proprium est, sed omnium animalium, quae in caelo, quae in terra, quae in mari nascuntur.*"

[4] This quotation is not identical with the *Digest* and *Institutes*. It follows the *Digest* more closely.

share law or, indeed, anything else, with the rest of the animate world.   We do not know the view of other animate creatures on the question of this association, but no less a person than Lord Bryce [1] has said that the acceptance of the doctrine of evolution tends to rehabilitate rather than annihilate Ulpian's generosity to brute creation.   Nevertheless it is but fair to say that this passage has caused jurists and commentators for many a century untold hours of time in an attempt to explain why animals should share with men in the law natural; and Suárez himself felt obliged to meet the question. Even Grotius, in his younger days, as is evidenced by the Commentary *On the Law of Prize*,[2] was generous to animals, but upon reflection he subsequently excludes them from natural law in his Three Books *On the Law of War and of Peace*.[3]

The question, although interesting, is unimportant for our present purpose and we need not here attempt to solve it; in any event, it could fairly be solved only by a conference of the parties in interest, which might be dangerous to the proponents of *homo sapiens*.

The proponents of Ulpian's view, having given the law natural to both men and animals, restricted the *jus gentium* to the human race, Suárez invoking, in behalf of this view, the statement from the *Digest* that the law of nations "is that used by the human race," [4] the distinction between the natural law and the *jus gentium* thus being that the latter "is common only to men in their mutual relations."   However, the writers show the two forms of law as closely related, for in a passage from the *Digest* [5] the *jus gentium* is considered to be "that law which natural reason has established for all mankind, and is uniformly observed by all men."   Upon this Suárez makes the penetrating comment that "thus it is clear that the *jus gentium* is held to be natural as well."   To what extent?   "In a special sense, peculiar to mankind."   For examples of its special and peculiar application to man, Suárez' authority is again the *Digest*: [6] "Piety toward God; obedience to one's progenitors and to one's country; the repulsion of violence and injury."

Admitting that there are actions "common . . . to men and to brutes," Suárez observes that they are of a material nature and that "the natural law forbids in man, many things from which the brutes are not restrained by natural instinct."   The difference between the two creations is the difference between instinct and reason.

While admitting the close relationship between the *jus gentium* and the natural law, Suárez rejects the views "of certain theologians" that the precepts of the *jus gentium* share with those of the natural law a quality of "intrinsic necessity."   This involves also the rejection of the opinion that

---

[1] Rt. Hon. James Bryce, *Studies in History and Jurisprudence: Essay on the Law of Nature* (New York and London, 1901), p. 588.   [2] Chap. ii.   [3] Bk. I, chap. i, n. 11, § 1.
[4] *Digest*, I. i. 1, § 4: "*Ius gentium est, quo gentes humanae utuntur.*"
[5] *Ibid.*, I. i. 9: "*quod vero naturalis ratio inter omnes homines constituit, id apud omnes peraeque custoditur vocaturque ius gentium.*"   [6] I. i. 2, 3.

the law of nations "differs from the natural law [only] in that the latter is revealed without reflection, or at least with the simplest sort thereof, while the precepts of the *jus gentium* are deduced by means of many and rather intricate inferences." To Suárez, the natural law was revealed by right reason, whether this right reason was of an instinctive nature or a process of profound reflection, while the precepts of the *jus gentium* arose not so much by a conscious reasoning as by unconscious usage.

But having rejected the view which credits the *jus gentium* with intrinsic necessity, Suárez, in his usual thorough manner, states his reasons for this rejection, the first being that numerous things spoken of as coming under the *jus gentium* nevertheless "are not characterized by the intrinsic necessity" in question, and to reinforce this statement, he gives as examples "division of property" and "slavery."

Still further to differentiate the *jus gentium* from the natural law and to give the law of nations its proper and distinct place in the legal hierarchy, he dissociates the *jus gentium* from the "primary moral principles" and their necessary conclusions, since, he continues, "all these principles and conclusions are included under the natural law strictly so-called"; and the confirmation of this is a truth which we, with Suárez, believe worthy of repetition—"that all the precepts written by God in the hearts of men, pertain to the natural law." The authority is also that which he had previously invoked, St. Paul's *Epistle to the Romans*,[1] to which Suárez adds— "all precepts which may clearly be inferred by reason from natural principles are written in human hearts," this time not contenting himself with a mere "therefore" but completing the syllogism for less acute minds than his: "therefore all such precepts pertain to the natural law."

On the other hand, the precepts of the *jus gentium* are not written in the human heart, but are "introduced by the free will and consent of mankind, whether in the whole human community or in the major portion thereof." Here we have a statement of vast implications, to be later elaborated by Suárez, but which he does not at the moment enlarge, contenting himself with dissociating these precepts from those "written in the hearts of men by the Author of Nature." And this enables him to add that the precepts of the *jus gentium* are "a part of the human, and not of the natural law."

But there was another distinction between the *jus gentium* and the natural law—that the precepts of the *jus gentium* "should follow, not as a manifest conclusion [from natural principles], but rather from some source less certain" and that therefore they are, as Suárez puts it, "dependent upon the intervention of human free-will and moral expediency, rather than upon necessity"—and necessity was a prime characteristic of the natural law. Suárez has many a time pointed out that natural law forbids a thing because

[1] ii. 14–15: "For when the Gentiles, who have not the law, do by nature those things that are of the law; these having not the law are a law to themselves.

"Who shew the work of the law written in their hearts, their conscience bearing witness to them, and their thoughts between themselves accusing, or also defining one another. . . .

it is evil or commands it because it is good.   Not so, however, with human law, including the *jus gentium*.   Herein lies another distinction; for under the *jus gentium* the subject-matter of the precept is neither good nor evil in itself but is made so by the command or prohibition of the *jus gentium*, and both command and prohibition are of human volition, not of divine origin.   In a word, the natural law is necessary in the nature of things; the *jus gentium* is advantageous, expedient, and even necessary, but only from the human point of view.

In the preceding passages Suárez has been distinguishing natural law in general from the *jus gentium*.   There are, however, two general divisions of natural law: the one concessive, the other mandatory; and there are likewise the same classifications of the *jus gentium*.   If one classification of the law natural is to be distinguished from the law of nations, so also is the other. Therefore let us pause a moment and consider these two classifications of the natural law.   Among the actions which properly take place under the natural law, there are many which are "permissible," that is to say, concessive and not mandatory or prescribed, nor, as Suárez points out, "are their contraries prohibited."   As examples of the concessive phase of natural law, Suárez refers to "the right to take a wife"—in this more enlightened age, he would have added, as well, the right to take a husband—or "the right to retain and preserve one's own liberty"; for action under either of these rights "is honorable and is permitted" but is not prescribed.   There is another two-fold classification of the natural law—one being positive or affirmative, that is, mandatory; the other negative in the sense that it is non-prohibitory, "as may be seen," Suárez says, "from the words of Covarruvias,"[1] a distinguished jurist and statesman of Spain, whose authority he invokes in this classification.

The concession or the prohibition may come from the natural law, but there may also be a concession which is derived from human law.   Nevertheless, if a right to do a certain act is once conceded by the human law, any obligation which results therefrom is, to quote Suárez, "natural," and that age-old maxim of the natural law comes into play—*Pacta sunt servanda*. The proof of this simple but immensely important statement is contained, says Suárez, speaking in the first person, in four examples from St. Isidore of Seville, "the examples concerning the occupation of abodes, buildings, fortifications and defences through just warfare."   Why should the law applicable be the law natural?   Because all these actions, Suárez says, are "permitted by the natural law," and an act permitted by the natural law implies a natural obligation upon the person "to refrain from violating such rights when possessed by another person," the obligation being under "natural legislation," that is to say, natural law.

Because of the fundamental nature of this passage, a mere paraphrase of it is not sufficient.   It should and indeed must be quoted in its entirety:

[1] On *Sext*, rule *peccatum*, pt. ii, § 11, n. 3.

In the first place, this is clearly proved, I think, through the first four examples of Isidore, that is, the examples concerning the occupation of abodes, buildings, fortifications and defenses through just warfare; for the law applying to all of these acts is the natural law, that is to say, they are all permitted by the natural law; and in like manner, the obligation incumbent upon one person, to refrain from violating such rights when possessed by another person, pertains to natural legislation.   It is only the actual exercise of these rights which may be said to come within the field of the *jus gentium*, by reason of the custom of all nations.   And this exercise of rights is a matter pertaining to fact, and not to law.

The right under a concession may, as we have seen, come from the natural law; but if the right under the law natural is concessive, the exercise of the right is volitional and human and therefore within the *jus gentium*.   There is, however, an obligation to refrain from violating the right in question, and this obligation, like the right itself, comes under natural law.   In a word, the natural law is both a source and a sanction for the right; and the putting of such a right into execution comes under the *jus gentium* only because it depends upon the human will, which has become crystallized, as it were, in what Suárez calls "the custom of all nations."

Suárez refers also to the eighth, ninth and tenth examples from St. Isidore, relating "to peace, truces and ambassadors"; for the conclusion of peace and truces and the sending of ambassadors are governed by rules arising from human agreement, but the power or the right to contract, and the obligation which may arise from the treaty or covenent or contract, or whatever form the agreement may take, demand this "good faith and justice" which, in Suárez' own words, "have regard to the law of nature." *Pacta sunt servanda.*

There are, however, rules regarding the exercise of these rights and powers —an exercise which is volitional on the part of men and nations; and such rules concerning the exercise of these rights, having been agreed upon by all or nearly all nations, are of the *jus gentium*.   But, continues Suárez with natural law uppermost in his mind as the wellspring, so to speak, of human law, "actual use" of these powers is not law; it is "the effect of law."   And the proof of this is simple and logical, as it is indisputable: "For the law under discussion"—meaning natural law—"does not spring from such use; on the contrary, the use has its source in the law."

By way of summarizing, Suárez concludes with certain fundamental distinctions between the *jus gentium* and the natural law, and as this summary forms a transition to the discussion of the agreement between the two, Suárez should speak in his own behalf and in his exact language:

From what has thus far been said, the conclusion seems to follow that the *jus gentium*, properly so-called, is not contained within the bounds of the natural law, but that, on the contrary, it differs essentially therefrom; for although it agrees with the natural law in many respects, nevertheless the two kinds of law are distinct from each other owing to their characteristic moral difference.

Now as to their agreement.   We again quote the language of Suárez; for what can be better than his own summary of his doctrine?

They agree, indeed, because, in the first place, both are in some manner common to all mankind.   And on this ground each may be called a law of nations (*gentium*), if we are to insist upon words alone.   The characteristic of being common to all nations is evident in the natural law, and for that reason the law of nature itself is called, in the *Digest* (I. i. 9), the law of nations (*jus gentium*)—as may be noted in the wording of many laws.   However, this name is more properly bestowed upon the system of law introduced by the custom of nations. On this point, consult the *Institutes* (I. ii, § 4 [I. ii, § 2]).

In the second place, the two kinds of law in question agree in that just as the subject-matter of the *jus gentium* has application to men alone, so also the subject-matter of the natural law is peculiar to mankind, either in its entirety, or in great part, as is, perhaps, sufficiently evident from what we have said in Chapter xvii.   Consequently, many examples which are placed by the jurists under the heading of the *jus gentium* because of this characteristic alone, belong only nominally to that system of law, strictly viewed. . . .

In the third place, the *jus gentium* and the natural law agree, in that both systems include precepts, prohibitions, and also concessions or permissions, as has been made sufficiently clear in Chapter xviii.

After having discussed not only the distinctions but also the points in which natural law and the *jus gentium* agree, Suárez passes to the points of difference between the two great systems.   In general, it may be said that the differences are fundamental and, though numerous, they may be combined into one all-embracing difference: the law of nature is a law of necessity; the *jus gentium* is a desirable law.   The one exists to meet the necessity; the other is made to conform to human desire.   Natural law is of a higher will—indeed, the highest of wills—whether it be in the phrase of the Greeks, "design in nature," or whether it be God, the Creator.   Man has no part in its formulation.   In the *jus gentium* human will not only enters but is the controlling factor—not the will of any one man and not the will of any number of human beings in isolation or in a single group, but the will of individuals grouped into states.   It is the law of many peoples, if not of all peoples; it is the law of many states, if not of all states.   Or, to express it in terms of man and society, it is the consensus of the will of humankind or the censensus of the international community.

Natural law, then, is of supernatural origin and it is immutable until human nature itself changes.   The *jus gentium* is based upon, and indeed is, the expression of the common will and desire of human beings; it is changeable as are their common will and desires, and grows, not out of the natural inherent necessity of human nature, but out of the necessities arising from organized society.

The all-embracing difference with which we have just dealt refers particularly to the affirmative precepts of both the law natural and the *jus gentium*.

There are, however, negative precepts.   In the law natural, a thing or an action is prohibited because it is inherently wrong in itself, whereas, as we have said (in the language of Suárez), the negative precepts of the *jus gentium* do not forbid anything on the ground that it is evil in itself.   Rather, he says, the *jus gentium* "not only points out what is evil, but constitutes

[the forbidden matter as] evil," with the result "that it does not forbid evil actions on the ground that they are evil, but prohibiting them, causes them to be evil." In this regard the two systems are as far apart as the North and the South Poles. These are indeed "real" differences and also "essential" differences. To sum it up in a word: "accordingly, in these ways, there is a distinction between the natural law and the *jus gentium.*"

The second difference pointed out by Suárez we have implied, but as Suárez states it expressly and briefly, it should be given in his own words: "The two systems under discussion," he goes on to say, "likewise differ in that the *jus gentium* cannot be immutable to the same degree as the natural law; for immutability springs from necessity, and therefore, that which is not equally necessary cannot be equally immutable, a point which will be expounded more fully in the following chapter." Here we have absolute universality, arising from universal necessity, and relative universality, arising from human necessity, that is, from the needs of society and therefore subject to change as society is subject to change.

But even when these "two systems of law seem to agree," as Suárez puts it, "they are not absolutely similar." The reason may seem to be evident, but it is conclusively so after Suárez' statement—"for in its universality and general acceptance by all peoples, the natural law is common to all, and only through error can it fail of observance in any place." On the contrary, however, "the *jus gentium* is not observed always by all nations, but [only] as a general rule by almost all: as Isidore states."

This is indeed an important statement, and the conclusion which Suárez draws is even as important: "Hence, that which is held, among some peoples, to be *jus gentium*, may elsewhere, and without any error, fail to be observed." We here have an admission that international law need not be so universal as natural law, because social necessities may differ from continent to continent, if not from state to state. Europe may have a series of policies separate and distinct from those of America; and as there may be what we Americans would call special rules of international law in Europe for European conditions, so there may be special rules of international law for American conditions. However, as the European conception of the law of nations was the original basis of international law, the exceptions to such law would of necessity deal with what we may call local conditions and differences in other parts of the world; so that, to the extent of these local differences, there might come into existence what could be, and indeed is, at times called, for example, an American international law, although the rules peculiar to it would be few in number and would be additions to, rather than derogations from, the general law of nations.

In a final statement on this phase of the subject Suárez more than implies another difference between the law natural and the *jus gentium.* "The natural law is that law which does not spring from human conjecture, but from the evidence of nature, as Cicero has pointed out." And the second

term of the syllogism: "Hence, every law that does not arise in this way is positive and human." The conclusion of this informal syllogism is so natural with Suárez and with the schoolmen that it frequently is not stated as such, in the hurry of writing: "And the *jus gentium* is of this latter variety, because it came into existence not through [natural] evidence, but through probability and the common judgment of mankind." Suárez ends with a "therefore," which we complete: Therefore the *jus gentium* is positive human law.

We now pass with Suárez to the differences between the *jus gentium* and the civil law, Suárez saying that the civil law has its precepts in written form, whereas those of the *jus gentium*—at least in his day—could be said to be unwritten. Again speaking of his day, the precepts of the *jus gentium* were "established through the customs, not of one or two states or provinces, but of all or nearly all nations." Here we have an all-important phrase, "of all or nearly all nations." A custom has to have a beginning, and that may be in the usage of one state, in which case it binds that state only and could appropriately be called a civil or national custom. The custom becomes international when more states adopt it, and if practised by many—though not necessarily all—states, it becomes a precept of the "*jus gentium* properly so-called." Thus isolated usage may grow into the custom of many, if not all, and the evidence of this general custom is the practice of nations. In a single sentence Suárez sums up the differences not only between the *jus gentium* and the natural law but also between the *jus gentium* and the civil law. The law of nations, he says, "differs from the natural law because it is based upon custom rather than upon nature; and it is to be distinguished likewise from civil law in its origin, basis and universal application." It is neither the law of a Supreme Being nor is it the law of emperor, of king, of prince or of legislature or other enacting body; it is, so far as custom is concerned, human usage and on a universal scale. Customs may, however, be local, in that they apply to a group of communities, and thus they deviate from the general rules of international law (as we may suppose in the case of Europe and America; for we of the Western World might have a custom, or a series of American customs, enlarging the content of international law in the Americas to the extent of the customs in question). This localization of international law, if the term be permitted, may also occur—oftener in our day than in Suárez' day—by the conclusion of treaties or conventions binding only the contracting parties, be they few or many. Often, however, the provisions of such treaties subsequently enter into the practice of many nations and to the extent of that practice, irrespective of the treaty, become general international law instead of regional law.

As this conception of what we may call regional international law is a matter of far-reaching implications, we feel justified in turning aside for a moment to consider a present movement which, unconsciously perhaps, has for its purpose the carrying into effect of this conception of Suárez.

Mr. Alejandro Alvarez, a distinguished publicist of the Republic of Chile, is the leading exponent, not merely in his own country but in America and in the world at large, of regional schools of international law. In an address on "The New International Law," delivered by him before the Grotius Society in 1929 and published in the *Transactions* of that society for 1930,[1] he says:

In the course of the nineteenth century, certain countries, notably the Great Powers, established special doctrines with respect to certain matters, in which their national interest ordinarily exerts a large influence. This is what is known as national International Law, or simply *schools* of International Law. These schools are the following: the French school, the Italian school, the German school, the North American school, the Russian or Slavic school, and the Japanese school. But all are attached to one or the other of the two great preceding schools: the United States with England form the *Anglo-Saxon school* and the other countries form the *Continental school*.

At the end of the nineteenth century, a great new school [of international law] commences to develop: the *Pan-American school*. It consists of doctrines relating both to American and to universal interests that are professed by all the nations of the New World, and that differ from those of the two preceding schools. It is American International Law.

Hence, the nations of America find themselves in a special situation with regard to International Law which I have already indicated more than once: namely, the United States professes the principles of the Anglo-Saxon school, while the Latin countries profess the principles of the Continental school; but, on the other hand, the United States and the Latin countries have a common body of doctrines which are peculiar to them.

In advance of the meeting of the International Commission of Jurists at Rio de Janeiro, held in 1927, the American Institute of International Law, created in 1912—of which Mr. Alvarez was one of the founders and Secretary-General—undertook the codification of "American International Law," at the request of the Governing Board of the Pan American Union, upon motion of its Chairman, then Secretary of States Hughes.[2] Some

[1] *Transactions of the Grotius Society* (London, 1930), Vol. 15, pp. 35, 44. For further expressions of Mr. Alvarez' views on the matter in hand, see *Le Droit International Américain* (Paris, 1910), note 3, pp. 5–6; *The Monroe Doctrine* (New York, 1924), pp. 26–31; *Considérations générales sur la codification du droit international américain* (Rio de Janeiro, 1927), pp. 15–30. For an opposite point of view, see Manoel Alvaro de Souza Sa Vianna, *De la non Existence d'un Droit International Américain* (Rio de Janeiro, 1912).

[2] The text of the Resolution of the Governing Board of the Pan American Union, adopted January 2, 1924, is as follows:

"Whereas the Fifth International Conference of American States adopted a vote of thanks for the results achieved by the American Institute of International Law; and

Whereas one of the purposes for which the American Institute of International Law has been established is to secure a more definite formulation of the rules of international law; and

Whereas the codification of the rules of international law is the most important task intrusted to the International Commission of Jurists; and

Whereas the labors of the American Institute of International Law will be of great service to the International Commission of Jurists in the fulfillment of the task assigned to it: Be it

Resolved by the governing board of the Pan American Union, To submit to the executive committee of the American Institute of International Law the desirability of holding a session of the institute in 1924 in order that the results of the deliberations of the institute may be submitted to the International Commission of Jurists at its meeting at Rio de Janeiro in 1925."—*Codification of American International Law* (Pan American Union, Washington, 1925), p. 15.

In the letter transmitting this unanimous resolution of the Governing Board, its Chairman, Secretary of State Hughes, said:

thirty projects were adopted by the American Institute at its session of 1924 in Lima, Peru.   From the second project, entitled "General Declarations," we quote the following paragraphs:[1]

2. The American Republics declare that matters pertaining especially to America should be regulated in our Continent in conformity with the principles of universal International Law, if that be possible, or by enlarging and developing those principles or creating new ones adapted to the special conditions existing on this Continent.

3. By American International Law is understood all of the institutions, principles, rules, doctrines, conventions, customs, and practices which, in the domain of international relations, are proper to the Republics of the New World.

The existence of this Law is due to the geographical, economic, and political conditions of the American Continent, to the manner in which the new Republics were formed and have entered the international community, and to the solidarity existing between them.

American International Law thus understood in no way tends to create an international system resulting in the separation of the Republics of this hemisphere from the world concert.

On March 2, 1925, Secretary Hughes, as Chairman of the Governing Board of the Pan American Union, laid before the Governing Board the various projects, saying:[2]

There are 30 of these projects covering a wide range of subjects dealing with the American international law of peace.   They represent the labors of distinguished jurists of this hemisphere. . . .   It is natural, as is pointed out by the executive committee of the American Institute of International Law, that the law to be applied by the American Republics should, in addition to the law universal, contain not a few rules of American origin and adapted to American exigencies, and that the old and the new, taken together, should constitute what may be called American international law, without derogation from the authority of the law which is applicable to all nations.

* * *

But as our French friends say, *retournons à nos moutons.*

Suárez himself regarded the foregoing distinctions between the *jus gentium* and the natural and civil law as of such importance that he reinforced them by citing and analyzing the best of authorities, the *Institutes* of Justinian and the *Etymologies* of St. Isidore, and joined to these the great name of St. Thomas.   "The foregoing seems," literally to quote Suárez, "in my judgment"—note the personal appeal—"to be the opinion of Justinian, as expressed in the *Institutes*. . . . 'The *jus gentium*, indeed, is common to all the human race, for because of imperative usage and human needs the nations of the earth have established certain laws for themselves.'"[3]   Upon

"The Commission of Jurists, provided for by the Santiago resolution, is called upon to perform a very great international service.   I feel convinced that in the performance of this service the American Institute of International Law can be most helpful.   I hope, therefore, that the suggestion submitted by the governing board of the Pan American Union may have the approval of the executive committee of the American Institute of International Law.   The establishment of such close cooperative relationship will serve to advance the work which the commission is called upon to perform and will thus bring us nearer to the accomplishment of the purpose for which the International Commission of Jurists was established."   *Ibid.*, at pp. 15–16.

[1] *Ibid.*, p. 26.   [2] *Ibid.*, pp. 1–2.   [3] *Institutes*, I. ii, §2.

this passage Suárez comments that "the phrases 'imperative usage' and 'have established' are to be carefully weighed; for the latter implies that the law in question was established, not by nature, but by men; and the phrase 'imperative usage' indicates that it was introduced, not by a written instrument, but through custom."

And St. Isidore,[1] he says, "holds the same view," defining natural law as "that which is common to all nations, in that it exists everywhere through natural instinct and not through any formal enactment." With this Suárez agrees, saying that "herein he supports our own statement" and indicates "that the *jus gentium* is not based upon natural instinct alone."

But this is not the only support which he derives from Isidore; for the latter, in a later passage in which he gives examples of the *jus gentium*, maintains that this system of law "is called the *jus gentium* because almost all nations make use of it."[2]

Now for the commentary of Suárez on these two passages. St. Isidore, he says, is here defining the *jus gentium*, "indicating that it is a system of law common to all nations, and constituted not through natural instinct alone, but through the usage of those nations." This, however, is but part of the penetrating comment. The rest has to do with a single word, but one of surpassing importance. "Neither," says Suárez, "should the little word 'almost' be lightly passed over, for it shows that there is no altogether intrinsic and natural necessity inherent in this law, and that it need not be absolutely common to all peoples, even aside from cases of ignorance or error; but that, on the contrary, it suffices if nearly all well ordered nations shall adopt that law." And to put the matter beyond dispute Suárez laconically adds that "St. Thomas appears to be of the same opinion."

It is evident that Suárez was deeply in earnest, because he uses in this connection the first person, disregarding the impersonal style in order to commit himself to these views, which he rightly thought were fundamental and incontestable.

But authorities, great as they were, were not enough for Suárez on these matters, the import of which none realized better than he. There were, he said, "several examples" upholding the same view, and the first of these was "the custom of receiving ambassadors under a law of immunity and security." This custom, "if considered in an absolute aspect, does not spring from any necessity of the natural law." This is a general statement and we would expect Suárez to furnish proof in the best scholastic manner: "Some particular community of men might fail to have within its territory, any ambassador of a foreign community; or it might be unwilling to admit such ambassadors"; nevertheless, the admittance of these representatives of foreign powers is an obligation imposed by the *jus gentium*. What would be the result of a failure to comply with this obligation? "To repudiate those ambassadors would be a sign of enmity, and a violation of the *jus gentium*,

---

[1] *Etymologies*, Bk. V., chap. iv.   [2] *Ibid.*, chap. vi.

although it would not be an injury committed in contravention of natural reason."

So it was in the time of Suárez. But to us of today, ambassadors and diplomatic agents are so much the rule that the refusal to admit them would seem to be unnatural.

But what is the conclusion which Suárez draws from his example of ambassadors? "Accordingly," he continues, "even assuming that they are indeed admitted on the basis of some implied agreement"—note that the agreement need not be express, but is equally binding if implied—"it would be contrary to the natural law not to respect their immunity." And the reason? "That such an act would be contrary to justice and plighted faith. Nevertheless, this assumption," Suárez adds, "and this implied agreement, in the case supposed, would have been introduced by the *jus gentium*." This passage is an interesting commentary on the reason why diplomatic agents were appointed, and on their immunity from the jurisdiction of the country to which they are accredited and in which they reside—an immunity which is necessary to them in the performance of their many and varied duties. Now the immunity arises out of an agreement, express or implied, between the parties, but the obligation to respect the immunity, whether express or implied, is necessary if the ambassador is to perform his official duties. Therefore, the disregard of the obligation is a violation of that good faith which is the very essence of the natural law and finds expression in the classic phrase, *Pacta sunt servanda*. A sanction is here implied, not for the agreement but for the obligation arising out of the agreement, to violate which is a violation of natural law, which violation renders the nation so violating it responsible. Why, we may ask. Because the natural law applies equally to all nations, and the nation disregarding it can not but be guilty before both God and man, irrespective of the existence or nonexistence of a municipal statute, which exists, however, today in all civilized nations—at least as regards the immunity of ambassadors and other diplomatic agents.

Suárez now furnishes a second example, also of a universal nature, that of "any contract or commercial agreement." In connection with this, there are three points to be distinguished: first, "the specific method of making the contract." This is a matter which "ordinarily pertains to civil law," and, as Suárez maintains, "is frequently decided in accordance with the will of the contracting parties," provided, of course, that their will "conflicts with no existing legal rule."

So much for the first point. The second is "the observance of the contract after it has been made." As we would expect, Suárez at once observes that this "pertains to the natural law." *Pacta sunt servanda*.

Now for the third point—"the liberty to contract commercial agreements with [any] man not actively hostile or unfriendly in sentiment"—or, as we would say today, "freedom to contract"—a freedom derived, Suárez in-

forms us, "from the *jus gentium*." But why should this be so? Because the making of such agreements is not "an obligation imposed by natural law considered in itself"—the action being one of volition—since "a state might conceivably exist in isolation and refuse to enter into commercial relations with another state, even without unfriendly feeling."

So much for the natural law on this point. "But," says Suárez, "it has been established by the *jus gentium* that commercial intercourse shall be free, and it would be a violation of that system of law if such intercourse were prohibited without reasonable cause." Here we have Suárez aligning himself with Victoria, who proclaimed not only that freedom of commercial intercourse was a natural right, but that the natural right could and should have a municipal sanction in case of its violation, and that if the sanction did not exist, the nation failing to comply with this international duty in this respect would be responsible in damages and liable to suit in the court of the prince.[1] Today the liability is the same, but the suit is in a Permanent Court of International Justice at The Hague.

In the Roman law, which Suárez knew so well, and in the parlance of the jurists, of the canonists, and of the theologians, the term *jus gentium* was used in a twofold sense; or, as he puts it, was viewed in two different aspects:

first, as the law which all the various peoples and nations ought to observe in their relations with each other.

This is the international law of which Suárez speaks as one of the founders, reaching back in origin through the centuries, and today the modern law of nations.

Now for the second of the two aspects of the *jus gentium*, which is

as a body of laws which individual states or kingdoms observe within their own borders, but which is called *jus gentium* because these laws are similar [in each instance] and are commonly accepted.

What is the difference between these two classes? Suárez answers this question immediately: "The first interpretation seems, in my opinion,"— he is here speaking in his own behalf—"to correspond most properly to the actual *jus gentium*"—again we interpolate, the modern law of nations—"as distinct from the civil law, in accordance with our exposition of the former."

What, now, of the second kind of *jus gentium*? It involves, in Suárez' definition, "certain precepts, usages, or modes of living, which do not, in themselves and directly, relate to all mankind"—as do the principles of international law proper—"neither do they have for their immediate end, so to speak, the harmonious fellowship and intercourse of all nations with respect to one another." The usages of this kind of *jus gentium* are, on the contrary, he continues, "administered in each state by its own courts,

[1] Francisco de Vitoria, *De Indis*, § III, nos. 1–6, Carnegie Institution edition above cited, pp. 151–4.

according to appropriate rules." In other words, although this law is essentially local law, applying within different localities, it is similar and may even be identical in form and provision. Indeed, Suárez himself continues that these provisions "are of such a nature that, in the use of similar customs or laws, almost all nations agree with one another," that is, we may say, all nations of the civilized world which have, or ought to have, a similar standard. If they are not identical, "at least, they resemble one another, at times in a generic manner and at times specifically, as it were."

Recurring now to the first aspect of the *jus gentium*, Suárez declares it as his opinion that it corresponds "most properly" to the law of nations, as such, "as distinct from the civil law," and to tie the matter up with what he has just said, he adds that "the examples mentioned above concerning ambassadors and commercial usage, also pertain to this first aspect."

But there were other matters which pertained to the *jus gentium* in the sense of the law of nations, and therefore Suárez refers next to "the law of war," which he considers likewise a part of international law, properly so called, "in so far as that law rests upon the power possessed by a given state or kingdom, for the punishment, avenging or reparation of any injury inflicted upon it by another state." This is, of course, the law of nations and the law of war of Victoria. War does not seem to Suárez to be inevitable; if it were, it would fall within the province of the natural law. The fact remains, however, that the power to make war might not have existed in an injured state, had men "established some other mode of vindication, or entrusted that power to some third prince and quasi-arbitrator with coercive power." Most wars are condemned within a few years after their conclusion; and at the present day we are attempting to condemn them before they happen, not only by outlawing war but by having at the disposal of the parties in dispute proper remedies, beginning with good offices and terminating with the Permanent Court of International Justice at The Hague, although none of the remedies is endowed with coercive power other than that of public opinion. Nevertheless, they may properly be counted as in direct line of descent from Suárez' "third prince and quasi-arbitrator."

But this peaceful procedure was, unfortunately, not in favor in Suárez' day, war being generally considered easier and more in conformity with nature, at least animal nature, and this being the case, the bellicose method of settling disputes, he would have us believe, "has been adopted by custom, and is just to the extent that it may not be rightfully resisted,"— meaning that in a just war, undertaken for the reparation of an injury received, the party who had committed the injury and resisted the just claims of what we may call the defendant state, was in the wrong. Without dwelling upon the matter—which is a separate topic, and amply covered by Suárez in his Disputation on Charity—the only justification for war, in the opinion of enlightened theologians, from St. Augustine down, was that between equal states there was not, and could not be, in the then state of affairs,

a court of the superior.   We of today have, as already indicated, solved the difficulty by creating a court of the superior, the superior in this instance being none other than the international community, and to this supreme tribunal all states of the world may appeal for a redress of their legal wrongs. It is not impossible that the future—less familiar than we with the past— may ask how enlightened theologians could ever have considered a resort to force as a permissible and even a just remedy.

We have seen that Suárez' *jus gentium* is made up very largely of custom. Nevertheless he was not unaware that treaties also came under the law of nations.   Indeed he expressly says, "treaties of peace and truces may be placed under the head of the *jus gentium*"—meaning, in the strict sense of the term, our modern law of nations.   And since the instruments themselves formed a part of the law of nations, so offers to make them, voluntary though they be, "should be heeded, and not refused, when duly presented, and for a reasonable cause."   But the obligation created by the voluntary agreement "pertains rather to the natural law," on the simple theory that good faith exists between nations as well as between individuals and therefore requires the execution of international as well as of individual contracts.

It is to be said that while a treaty, as an agreement, is under the law of nations, good faith is a principle—indeed it is a first principle—of the natural law; therefore the violation of the obligation created by the treaty is a breach not only of international but of the natural law.   Such a violation of the natural law is an offense not merely against the nation involved but against all nations, as all are bound by and are beneficiaries under the law natural, and it is a right of every nation to insist that the law of nature should be respected and that therefore the obligation under the law of nations— which "pertains to the natural law," as Suárez says—should be observed in its entirety.   Now an obligation on the part of one nation implies a right on the part of another, and the right, like the obligation correlative with it, is under the protection of the law natural.   It follows, therefore, that if the rights of one nation under natural law are violated, then the rights of all nations under natural law are endangered and the maxim *Pacta sunt servanda* becomes but empty words.

Let us, however, recur for a moment to another form of obligation in connection with treaties of peace,—a matter which Suárez has already mentioned—that of agreeing to negotiate them when an offer is made.   The compliance with such an offer "is to a great degree in harmony with natural reason."   However, in his opinion, it receives "additional support from custom itself," and not only from custom but also "from the law of nations, thus becoming a matter of strict obligation."   This is of no small importance, for many and many a war would have been terminated in its earlier stages had the acceptance of an offer of peaceful settlement been considered as compulsory.

These observations lead up to a series of conclusions which, taken together,

are not only a classic but perhaps the most memorable passage in the history of the law of nations.   It has been customary for writers on international law to quote the passage in its entirety, but, while this may the better display its literary beauty, it nevertheless fails to disclose its many unsuspected implications.   Therefore we shall quote it sentence by sentence.

1. The rational basis of this branch of law [the law of nations], indeed, consists in the fact that the human race, howsoever many the various peoples and kingdoms into which it may be divided, always preserves a certain unity not only as a species, but also, as it were, a moral and political unity called for by the natural precept of mutual love and mercy, which applies to all, even to strangers of any nation.

This is a suggestion of the international community, and the reason why this community exists is to be found in the existence of states, separate and independent of one another and yet linked one to the other.   It is a political community, because the states are political groups of human beings; it is a social community, because human beings are essentially social and unite in society; and it is a moral community, and will always be such, because the progress of man is measured by his conception and understanding of the moral law, towards whose perfection the path of civilization leads him.

2. Therefore, although a given sovereign state, commonwealth, or kingdom, may constitute a perfect community in itself, consisting of its own members, nevertheless, each one of these states is also, in a certain sense, and viewed in relation to the human race, a member of that universal society; for never are these states, when standing alone, so self-sufficient that they do not require some mutual assistance, association and intercourse, at times for their greater welfare and advantage, but at other times because also of some moral necessity or lack, as is clear from experience.

There is, it is believed, no better statement of the interdependence of nations to be found in the books, and comment would be as impertinent as it is superfluous.

3. Consequently, such communities have need of some system of law whereby they may be directed and properly ordered with regard to this kind of intercourse and association; and although this law is in large measure provided by natural reason, it is not provided in sufficient measure and in a direct manner, with respect to all matters; therefore, it was possible for certain special rules of law to be introduced through the practice of these same nations.

This implies that the law of nations reinforces and extends the law of nature, which is revealed through natural reason.   And is it too much to hope that one day, however far in the future it may be, the law of nations may respond as does the law natural to the everlasting fundamentals of our human nature, which can not change without our ceasing to be enlightened men and women?

4. For just as in one state or province law is introduced by custom; so among the human race as a whole it was possible for laws to be introduced by the habitual conduct of nations, and all the more because the matters comprised within this latter system of law are few, and very closely related to the natural law, and most easily deduced therefrom in a manner so advantageous and so in harmony with nature itself, that while this derivation [of the law of nations from the natural law] may not be self-evident, that is, not essentially and absolutely

required for moral rectitude, it is nevertheless quite in accord with nature, and universally acceptable for its own sake.

Here we have the origin, the process and the consequence of lawmaking in and for the international community. Is this not the emanation of a noble mind and of a great heart, and the hope of the world—that it may be governed in the future, as never in the past, by the high standard of right reason?

It would be scant courtesy to criticize Suárez by any other than the highest standard. With this in mind, and for the sake of comparison, we reproduce again in this connection a passage from Victoria's Reading *On the Civil Power*,[1] setting forth his conception of an international community:

International law has not only the force of a pact and agreement among men, but also the force of a law; for the world as a whole, being in a way one single state, has the power to create laws that are just and fitting for all persons, as are the rules of international law. Consequently, it is clear that they who violate these international rules, whether in peace or in war, commit a mortal sin; moreover, in the gravest matters, such as the inviolability of ambassadors, it is not permissible for one country to refuse to be bound by international law, the latter having been established by the authority of the whole world.

It is not for us to compare the passages from a moral standpoint. Nor is it our purpose to consider them as literature, although they are both admirable, with the scales inclining, at least in our opinion, towards Victoria. If the two passages, however, be compared from the standpoint of international law, the statement of Suárez is seen to lack that sense of ultimate completeness which always seems to have been in the mind of Victoria; his is not merely an international community with law, but it is an international community with the power to create law and to punish the violations of that law. It may well be that the presence of law in Suárez' community implies both the right consciously to create and the power to preserve that law inviolate; but neither the right nor the power are express, as in the case of Francis of Victoria's international community. For does not Victoria say expressly that the *jus gentium* has "the force of a pact and agreement among men"? Whereas Suárez implies in the succeeding chapter of this very book that the law of nations may have been introduced simply through "usage and tradition, . . . and without any special and simultaneous compact or agreement on the part of all peoples." This conception of Suárez looks to an inorganic association; Victoria's conception looks to an organized society, with a law of nations having the force of a pact, the obligations of which are enforceable, not merely under the law of nations but under the natural law.

Our Daniel Webster, as Secretary of State, had in mind—unconsciously, it may be—the Victorian conception of a pact and an agreement; for his international community is the organic community of Victoria rather than the inorganic community of Suárez, as appears from an instruction from

[1] *De Potestate Civili*, § 21. A translation of this *Relectio* is printed in Scott, *The Spanish Origin of International Law—Part I, Francisco de Vitoria and His Law of Nations*, above cited, Appendix C, pp. xxi–lxii.

Mr. Webster, as Secretary of State, to Mr. Thompson, Minister to Mexico, under date of April 15, 1842. "Every nation," Secretary Webster says, "on being received . . . into the circle of civilized governments, must understand that she not only attains rights of sovereignty and the dignity of national character, but that she binds herself also to the strict and faithful observance"—we interpolate, *Pacta sunt servanda*—"of all those principles, laws, and usages which have obtained currency among civilized states."[1]

To return to Suárez' *jus gentium*, properly so called. How did it come into being, or, rather, the question which he has in mind is, how could it have come into being? To which he answers that it "could have been gradually introduced throughout the whole world . . . simply through usage and tradition," and, enlarging upon and emphasizing the matter, he adds, "by means of tradition, propagation and mutual imitation among the nations." And fundamental though it is, this law, as we have seen, could have been introduced in Suárez' conception of the international community "without any special and simultaneous contract or agreement on the part of all peoples." With Victoria, as has been indicated, the international community is by the very existence of states an organic community, with the power to make laws to prevent the violation of the obligations which every state has by reason of its existence and membership in the community. With Suárez, the law of the international community was simply the product of "usage and tradition" rather than of "pact and agreement" among nations.

But to continue our analysis of Suárez' *jus gentium*, which, in its various parts, "has such a close relationship to nature, and is so advantageous to all nations, individually and collectively, that it has grown almost by natural process with the growth of the human race." Had the body of law in question been indispensable in the nature of things, it would have been natural law. It was not thus indispensable but it was and is "advantageous", not merely to one nation but to all nations, whether considered "individually" or "collectively", and its growth might therefore be considered as well-nigh a natural process by those who looked at results rather than at the process. Although it is not natural law, it exists, Suárez points out, like natural law, in unwritten form. The reason for his view? The law of nations is not dictated by a legislator but "has, on the contrary, waxed strong through custom." Today, we may add, that which was formerly unwritten is, to an ever greater extent, becoming written international law.

Passing now from the *jus gentium*, properly so called, to the term as used by Suárez in the second sense, that is to say, as denoting the existence of uniform laws in the various states, "the source of the great similarity of the forms in which it exists" is, he says, "easy to explain." It was indeed so to him but not to preceding generations, inasmuch as the term *jus gentium*

[1] John Bassett Moore, *A Digest of International Law* (Washington, 1906), Vol. I, p. 5.

appears to have been used by Roman lawyers as synonymous with the natural law, which the peoples of all states were credited with using. The Romans therefore introduced and applied this *jus gentium*, which we would call natural law, to the transactions of foreigners settled among them, who could not use the civil law of the Romans, because its application was limited to the Romans themselves. The "new wine in old bottles" had the traditional result.

But to Suárez and his explanation of the similarity in local laws. "The resemblance," he says, "is not always perfect," as it consists "only in a general and common rational basis." Whence and what is this common basis? While it is "not derived from natural law," it is "so closely related" to it and is "so thoroughly in accord or harmony with nature that through it the individual nations could easily have been led to adopt the rules in question." And a further and final explanation is to be found in "tradition, and a mutual imitation," which Suárez supposes began with the beginning of the human race.

Returning now to the *jus gentium* properly so called, Suárez invokes the very words of St. Thomas, "that the precepts of the *jus gentium* are conclusions drawn from principles of the natural law," differing, therefore, from the precepts of the civil law, which are not, as in the case of the *jus gentium*, "general conclusions" but "specific applications of the natural law." Is there, in fact, any difference in this respect between the civil law and the *jus gentium* in its primary sense? The answer which Suárez makes to this question is the opinion of Soto, to the effect that the rules of the *jus gentium* are here considered as general conclusions of the law natural, "not in an absolute sense and by necessary inference, but in comparison with the specific applications of civil and private law."

Now in the civil and private law, one of two events must occur, Suárez says, and the first is that "a merely arbitrary specific application is made of the sort concerning which it is said that, 'Whatever pleases the prince has the force of law.'" Given the conception of the state in which the majority controls the prince, this would seem to be strange doctrine for Suárez to profess. But he explains in the succeeding clause that he is not here supporting the unlimited arbitrary power of the prince, for he declares that an application in such terms is not due to the fact that the prince's will "alone suffices as a rational basis, but because that particular decision might reasonably have taken one of various forms." Then, too, "there is frequently no ground on which one form"—of specific application—"should be preferred to another," and it is for this reason alone that the decision is said to be made by the princely will "rather than in accordance with reason."

Now the second of the events arises in a situation calling for a choice, in which case reason is weighed with reference to particular and material circumstances, so that, as Suárez puts it, "the decision thus results from the

surrounding circumstances rather than from the substance of the matter in hand." Again we meet, in classic language, a famous colloquial expression "circumstances alter cases."

So much for the precepts of the civil and private law.

Now for the law of nations, the precepts of which are, as Suárez has already said, "of a more general character." Why? Because, as the *jus gentium* is the law of all, or of most nations, it must perforce take into consideration "the welfare of all nature," and since it is, as Suárez has so often pointed out, very closely related to the law of nature, it must be in conformity with nature's "primary and universal principles." Hence it is that such precepts are Suárez' conception of what are properly called "conclusions drawn from natural principles"; but this conception is supported by a further and unanswerable argument—that "their appropriate character and moral value are immediately made manifest by the force of natural reason; an appropriateness and value which have induced men to introduce the customs in question (as the Emperor Justinian has said) more because of the pressure of necessity than because of their own wills." The difference here is between an absolute, and a controlled and human necessity.

In relation to law in general, what then, is the character of the law of nations? This is not an impertinent question, for even to this day there survives an argument as to the legal nature of international law. But to Suárez, the greatest legal philosopher of his day, and, as a great authority puts it, the "prince of modern jurists," the matter was not open to argument. To him the *jus gentium* had every characteristic of true law. "We conclude," he says, "that equity and justice must be observed in the precepts of the *jus gentium*." Why? To which question, implicit in his argument, he answers: "For such observance is included in the rational basis of every true law, . . . and the rules pertaining to the *jus gentium* are indeed true law." But this was not the whole of Suárez' conception of human laws which, as he has repeatedly said before, are laws only if and in so far as they are in conformity with the natural law. The rules of the *jus gentium*, he continues, are "more closely related to the natural law than are those of civil law." At which point we meet the "therefore" of the syllogism, introducing a conclusion from his fellow-countryman Covarruvias, "it is impossible that these precepts of the *jus gentium* should be contrary to natural equity." And we add in our own behalf that this passage should be inscribed in letters of gold in every Ministry of Foreign Affairs of every state of the international community. If this were done, international law would become, through the ages, a human inspiration as well as a human necessity, not only truly legal but as moral as it is admittedly social.

The great Victoria was not averse to corollaries; indeed, we have quoted on a previous page one of the very greatest of his corollaries—that upon which the municipal sanction of the law of nations depends. In this respect, as well as in others, Suárez was like the *maestro*, although he did not

invariably label his corollaries as corollaries.   In the present instance, a corollary is inferred by Suárez from the preceding discussion and it is as important as any of his text.   The corollary is "that the *jus gentium* is subject to change, in so far as it is dependent upon the consent of men," differing in this respect, as repeatedly said, from natural law.

Now there are in the *jus gentium* two elements.   One is the relationship to or derivation from natural law—and to the extent that the law of nations is thus a part of the natural law, its rules may partake of the immutability of the law natural.   And the other element is human consent.   In so far as this second element is involved, the making and unmaking of the law of nations lies within the power of man.   But this power to change the law of nations is to be exercised by society in general or by the majority of the international community, as, in the conception of Suárez, this law was largely a matter of universal custom.   The power, however, is not to be exercised by private authority, except in so far as the individual may, if he so desires, renounce rights which are conceded to him by the law of nations, just as rights conceded or permitted by the law of nature may also be renounced.   As in Suárez' day it was possible for "a given person" to "make himself a slave by renouncing his natural liberty," so also, under the law of nations, "a religious may renounce the ownership of temporal goods, and even the capacity for such ownership."   But such changes, whether in the law of nature or of nations involve only what Suárez calls "negative" precepts, that is, those which permit, but do not positively require, or prohibit, an act—as in the case of a "religious" renouncing the natural right to take a wife.   Indeed the same right of renunciation exists as regards rights "individually granted by the civil or canon law."

What, however, of the prohibitions, or positive precepts of the *jus gentium*?   On what ground are they subject to change when, as we know, the positive precepts of the natural law are immutable?   The reason here is easy to understand, inasmuch as things are intrinsically good or bad under natural law, whereas under the law of nations they are only good or bad in so far as the law makes them so.

There is a second reason, which also goes to the root of things: "the obligation imposed by the *jus gentium*," as Suárez holds, "does not spring from reason alone, apart from human obligation of every sort."   If it did, the *jus gentium* would be nothing more nor less than the natural law in the Anglo-Saxon guise of the rule of reason.   Nor does the fact that the law of nations "has its source in general custom" alter the view, because custom is not essentially a thing of reason.

It would be inconsistent with reason if the law of nature should be subject to change, since it is the perfection of reason; but the law of nations, being man-made, is to that extent imperfect, because man's reason is imperfect, and therefore "it is not absolutely inconsistent with reason that the said law should be subjected to change."   There is, however, an extremely im-

portant proviso to this concession on the part of Suárez—that the change must "be made on sufficient authority." This power to change the law of nations was likewise conceded by Victoria, with the same proviso, but expressed in more perfect form, because Victoria was dealing not only with changes in the law of nations but with the very formation of that law. Instead of the "sufficient authority" of Suárez, the authority of Victoria, in his dissertation *On the Indians*, was that of the "consensus of the greater part of the whole world, especially in behalf of the common good of all,"[1] a passage which recalls the classic language of the Reading *On the Civil Power*, in the twenty-first section, that international law has been established "by the authority of the whole world."[2] Therefore it would not be permissible for one group of nations or a minority of nations to attempt to establish an international law for the whole world, although they may establish a special rule of conduct for their own guidance and to meet their own special conditions. Neither may they derogate from the generally established international law, since, as Victoria says, "it is not permissible for one country to refuse to be bound by international law."[3]

There was a difference in this respect, however, between the *jus gentium* proper and the secondary *jus gentium* in the sense of the civil law common to several or many nations, and Suárez brings out the distinction with such clearness that it can not possibly be stated better than in his own words: "In this connection, I must note, furthermore, that a given change may be effected in the *jus gentium* in one way, with respect to that phase of the said law which is merely in that several nations agree upon the suitability of certain precepts." What is the process involved in such a change? This *jus gentium*, which is "intrinsically . . . nothing more or less than civil law," can be "changed by an individual kingdom or state" at its will, but only, of course, "to an extent affecting that state alone." So much for the *jus gentium* used with respect to the law not of nations but common to certain nations. What, now, of the *jus gentium* or law of nations proper? "When one is dealing with that phase of the *jus gentium* [law of nations], which is common owing to the usage and customs of [all] nations, in so far as there exists among them any fellowship or intercourse," then, says Suárez, "changes are far more difficult." This is because the *jus gentium* in its primary sense involves law common to all nations and appears to have been introduced by the authority of all. "So that," continues Suárez, "it may not be annulled without universal consent." Here the two great luminaries of the Spanish School of International Law are in accord.

However, as Suárez has repeatedly said, a change in the law of nations would not be inconsistent with reason, and in the present passage dealing with this subject, the doctrine of mutability in international law has received its classic form and perfection. "Nevertheless," he goes on to say, "there

---

[1] *De Indis*, Section III, no. 4, Carnegie Institution edition above cited, p. 153.
[2] *De Potestate Civili*, loc. cit.   [3] *Ibid.*

would be no inherent obstacle to change in the subject-matter of such law, if all nations should agree to the alteration, or if a custom contrary to [some established rule of this law of nations] should gradually come into practice and prevail." However, such an event, he concludes, "although it might be conceived of, as not contrary to reason, yet seems impossible, practically speaking." Suárez does not mean that international law may not under certain conditions, and as an exception to his general rule, be changed by a state with reference to its own subjects, such a change affecting that state, and that state alone. However, this is dangerous doctrine, for if international law is the law universal, then the citizens and subjects of every state should have a right to its protection; and the circumstances must be special indeed to justify an attempt on the part of any nation to change the law of nations, even on its own behalf, especially if the change abolishes, restricts, or reduces a right acquired under, and therefore guaranteed by, the law of nations. But having thus questioned, and as it were, limited the doctrine, let us quote Suárez' exact words, both as to the exception and the example: "In another sense, a given community may ordain that, within its own territory and among its own subjects, the law in question shall not be observed, such an instance being conceivable and practical.[1] For it was thus that the rule of the *jus gentium* [law of nations] as to the enslavement of prisoners taken in a just war, was changed in the Church." In the example, the change, it is to be said, neither abolishes, restricts, nor reduces, but rather increases, the rights of human beings.

Civil law, Suárez has shown, is readily subject to change, and he now adds that it is "subject to change in its entirety," and herein he points out an important difference between it and the *jus gentium;* for the latter, he continues, "is said to be subject to change, not in the whole, but in part." The reason for this distinction is that it does not relate to "an absolute power of change, . . . that is, not to the mutable nature of these two bodies of law themselves," since, in so far as this quality is concerned, both are "inherently mutable." The distinction is rather "in accordance with the moral power and usage of men." In point of fact, Suárez declares the distinction is of a somewhat limited nature, since neither the law of nations nor the civil law "is mutable, in a general sense," the implication being that it would not be possible for all the peoples of the world to agree at the same time upon the complete change or abolition of either form of law. Thus the civil law, in the case of a particular precept, may be mutable without qualification, for the reason that the civil law is not universal, "whereas," Suárez holds, the precepts "of the *jus gentium* may be abrogated only in part." The reason for this limitation on change in or abrogation of the *jus gentium* Suárez has

---

[1] In the General Treaty of Inter-American Arbitration, concluded at Washington, January 5, 1929, the second Article reads in part as follows:

"There are excepted from the stipulations of the treaty the following controversies:
(a) Those which are within the domestic jurisdiction of any of the Parties to the dispute and are not controlled by international law; . . .

already indicated, stating that it can occur only through the agreement of "all nations," or through general custom. And if such unanimity, or near unanimity, is required for the change or abrogation of a single precept of the law of nations, it is inconceivable that the law as a whole should become subject to change or abolition. Even if it were conceivable or possible to deprive the states of the world of the common law of nations at one fell blow, it would be impossible for them to live without law; indeed, it would be well-nigh impossible for them to create a new *jus gentium*, as it were, offhand. The result could but be a world of anarchy, and not of law.

* * *

The thirty-second chapter of the third book of the tractate *De Legibus ac Deo Legislatore* is a formal answer to the query "whether the municipal laws of any kingdom or domain are binding on the men of that domain when they are dwelling outside its territorial limits."

In the first place Suárez states that the question involves four subdivisions—and in our own behalf we may add that it opens up the entire question of jurisdiction and the exterritoriality of law. As a preliminary step he indicates the way in which a person "may be related to a given domain or diocese," for Suárez, great as a jurist, was first and foremost a churchman. In the first subdivision, the type of relation to the domain in question is "as a permanent inhabitant" of that domain, one who, in other words, is physically dwelling in the country. This relationship is ordinarily indicated by the unqualified term "inhabitant". In the second, says Suárez, "at the opposite extreme," is the person "who has neither of these relations with the domain in question," that is to say, who is neither an inhabitant nor possesses a fixed dwelling place in the country. The third subdivision relates to "a permanent inhabitant" in the country, one "having his domicile therein," but who is "dwelling abroad at the time." Finally, there is a fourth category and Suárez designates as a member of this "a temporary denizen of the said domain" but one who has, however, "neither domicile nor origin therein,"—we would say a "transient."

We may eliminate with Suárez the first and second of what he calls the "situations"; for the first deals with the national always present within the country, and the second deals with the national always absent from the country. In the first case, therefore, the question of the binding obligation of the law is obvious, and in the second, as Suárez says, "it is clear that there is no possibility of legal obligation," because the national in this case is completely and permanently outside the jurisdiction of his country, and there is "no title existing under which the status of a subject may be imposed." Suárez here seems to mean by the "status of a subject," not the status of nationality as such but rather that of allegiance begotten of actual presence in the country of the prince. Therefore it is that Suárez devotes most of his attention to what he calls "the third and fourth points."

First of all he considers the question which he has stated at the beginning

of the chapter in its relation to the third of the classes which he has described, and a person of this class, "although he is at the time living or
traveling outside the boundaries of his own state, always remains a subject,"
provided that "he does not change his domicile." We thus see that in
Suárez' day, as in our own, the question of domicile was a thorny but important one in relation to matters of nationality, allegiance and jurisdiction.

In this connection Suárez refers to "the saying that the law binds all subjects and all parts of the community"; and from this point of view the law is
binding in the case in question. Now there was confirmation of this in considering the opposite side of the picture, namely, the case of the inhabitant
of some other domain who, "while dwelling in this one"—the kingdom under
consideration—"is not bound to observe the laws of the latter kingdom, a
fact which seems to be expressly defined in the Canon law", but a fact which
Suárez would accept, be it said, only on condition that the inhabitant in
question be considered as "under the obligation of observing the laws of his
own domain"; for if this were not the case, an anomalous situation would
arise in which the foreign inhabitant dwelling in the kingdom which Suárez
has in mind "would be free, solely on account of his absence, from the obligation of obeying the laws of either country," and this situation he rightly
characterizes as "absurd".

Suárez, as we have said, was a theologian dealing with lay questions, and
it was but natural that he should frequently rely upon theological examples.
In this particular section he confirms the general principle by illustrations
drawn from the Church, especially that of persons in a diocese subject to the
jurisdiction of the Bishop as distinct from inhabitants of the territory subject
to the Prince. In other words, Suárez invokes both the temporal and the
spiritual law, as the matter in hand may suggest.

In the present instance, the first confirmation is, as we have seen, a lay
example. To clinch the matter, however, Suárez invokes the authority of
his Church and uses a clerical illustration. He supposes that "a bishop
makes a rule" for a diocese, requiring that persons within the diocese and
subject to his jurisdiction, "who enjoy a benefice must reside therein during
a given period of time under pain of a given punishment or censure." If this
is the case, the bishop "so binds the holders of such benefices, wherever they
may be, that if they do not return to the diocese within the prescribed time,"
they suffer a penalty. This he lays down as a general rule, subject to the
exception that the offending person is neither ignorant of the rule nor unable
to comply with it. The result is that such "a provincial statute is binding
upon those belonging to a diocese, even while they are traveling elsewhere";
and the conclusion, applicable alike to civil as to ecclesiastical law, is that
"the same is true of any similar law."

It might be, and indeed it was not infrequently stated, Suárez admits—on
the basis of reading equalled by few, if any, in his order—"that no law is
binding outside the limits of the country of the lord or prince by whom it is

decreed," from which it follows that "the inhabitants of that country, generally speaking, do not sin if they violate the law in question while they are outside of this territory." "Such," according to Suarez, was "the common opinion of the Doctors." This conclusion, he informs us, is deduced from a passage in *Sext*,[1] according to which a person "living outside a particular diocese," who disobeyed a law, although made by the bishop thereof, did not "incur the sentence stipulated for that law." To this conclusion, however, Suárez had a ready and an unanswerable reply; it was to the effect that "in the passage under discussion, the reference is not to the binding authority of the law, but rather to the censure," or, as a layman of our day would say—to the penalty. That is to say, the law is none the less applicable to the individual because he is outside of the jurisdiction of the country, but the penalty can not be imposed until he returns. The question, therefore, is one of jurisdiction. Suárez, however, states the matter in words that can not be paraphrased and therefore he must, in this, as in many other instances, speak in his own behalf: "for the imposition of a censure pertains not to the directive"—that is to say, to the commanding— "but to the coercive power of the law." This is because "the superior or judge may not punish outside of the territory, although he may issue orders and impose obligations." In other words, the power of the superior in the case of the subject living outside his territory is limited to the issuing of orders and the imposing of obligations, but the superior may not penalize the failure to obey or fulfil the orders.

As bearing upon this phase of the question Suárez analyzes a decision of the Pope that *he who declares a law may be disobeyed with impunity outside his own territory*, Suárez adding that a declaration of a law is "the same as passing sentence [upon its violation]." But "the intention of the Pope, without doubt, was to assert that the statute in question was not [actually] violated by the subject in the situation posited." The reasons are twofold. The sovereign, in this or any other case, could not impose a penalty outside of his own jurisdiction and if he attempted to do so, the result would be not only that the provision concerning a penalty would be invalid, but that the actual provision of the law itself would have no force as regards the subject outside his jurisdiction. In other words, as far as the absent subject was concerned the penalty would be void and likewise the law. This interpretation of the Pope's decision Suárez appropriately applies to the Church, "so that the person who, under the supposed circumstances does not obey the statute, is not contumaciously disobedient to the Church," and as a logical conclusion this is furthermore "an indication that the person in question is not bound by that statute, even with respect to its directive force." The

---

[1] I. ii. 2. *Sext* (or *Liber Sextus Decretalium*) is the sixth book of the *Decretals* (*Corpus Juris Canonici*), being an addition to the collection of five books of *Decretals* compiled by Gregory IX. The *Sext* was prepared by a committee of canonists under Pope Boniface VIII, and was published in 1298. It includes papal constitutions subsequent to 1234, notably decrees of the two oecumenical councils of Lyons.

schoolman, in the best sense of the term, appears in the succeeding sentence, in which Suárez sets forth his conclusion—and a very important one for him as a Churchman and for the Christian world of the Catholic persuasion: "The truth of the antecedent is evident," he says, "since if the said subject were contumacious he might accordingly be excommunicated, and consequently would incur a legal censure. For excommunication," in what Suárez calls "the more probable opinion," could be inflicted upon an absent subject "dwelling in a foreign territory." Therefore the conclusion to be drawn from the Pope's statement is that just as the liability to a censure—that is, a penalty—"does not bind an absent person, neither does a law."

This, however, is the temporal phase. How about the conscience? "Although the statute in question may have been published without any provision as to censure or penalty, but simply with the force of a directive law binding in conscience, nevertheless it will not be binding upon absent subjects." But suppose an attempt were made to add a censure to the law? Still it would not be binding. Why? Because "its power to lay an obligation upon the conscience is not enlarged [or diminished] by reason of the censure." Why should this be so? The matter is important and indeed fundamental. "[The imposition of] a censure rather assumes the existence of jurisdiction and the power to bind; and when the provision for a censure is added, the jurisdiction [of the law] is not for that reason diminished or restricted." Neither, we may add in our own behalf, is the jurisdiction of the law extended by reason of the addition of a penalty, for jurisdiction is exercisable within, and only within, the domain of the government, whether it be territorial or spiritual, to which the person involved is subject.

There is a relation of measure between the jurisdiction and the domain; for the one may not be extended beyond the bounds of the other. However, Suárez continues, "all the authorities"—in this as well as in other cases—"do not agree as to the rational basis for the assertion in question." Some seek to justify the conclusion to which they come on the ground that the intent of the legislator was merely to "bind the subjects living within his own territory." Some opponents contended, moreover, that in this case the conclusion which "we"—meaning Suárez—"have laid down is true, only if the law is couched in general terms, since in that case, no other—that is to say, no more extensive—intent on the part of the lawmaker, is expressed; and therefore, if the legislator declares in express terms that he wishes to bind [all] subjects, wherever they may be, then" according to dissenting opinion, "the law is binding even upon subjects outside of the territory." However, Suárez meets this argument by referring again to the decision of the Pope which he had just cited, that "he who declares a law may be disobeyed with impunity outside his own territory," on which Suárez comments that the words of the Papal text "indicate a defect not merely of will, but also of power, a fact which is self-evident," but for which

he nevertheless invokes the *Digest*[1] and "the commentators," who are "commonly agreed upon this point."

The conclusion of Suárez would seem to be sufficiently clear, but the matter was so important, so far-reaching and fundamental that, having stated and met the reasons set forth by the dissenters, he now proceeds to give in unequivocal terms the true reasons for the conclusions which he has maintained—"the jurisdiction of any one state or prince does not include the power of making laws which shall be valid outside the state or kingdom." This is the fact, but Suárez was not content with fact unless expressed in terms of philosophy and therefore he implies a philosophical analogy. "Just as in philosophy," he says, "we are accustomed to say that an action does not continue outside its sphere of activity, owing surely to a defect of power and not of will; even so the activity of jurisdiction in the making of any law is limited to a [specific] territory, and hence"—the inevitable conclusion of the schoolman—"that law is not binding outside those territorial limits." And with another "therefore" he ends the entire discussion: "it is clearly to be inferred, that the lawgiver can not bind a subject outside the existing boundaries [of the state], even if he has the specific intention of doing so and expressly states that intention in the words of his law."

We now come to a mooted question which Suárez proceeds to discuss: "When a prince may punish a delinquent subject outside of his own territory." The conclusion which Suárez has just reached should in general, he maintains, be considered "as referring to the peculiar directive obligation imposed by law upon the conscience," this being the "proper and immediate effect of law." But if one were considering the matter from the viewpoint of "coercion by means of a penalty, it is the opinion of the jurists that when a subject has committed a crime outside of the state," the prince might inflict a punishment upon him only under certain specific circumstances; that is to say, when the penalty was applicable, not in the place where the crime was committed—namely, outside of the prince's jurisdiction—but only after the erring subject has returned to the realm of the prince. The penalty is thus not, as Suárez says, "imposed *ipso jure*," but its imposition is contingent upon the subject's return to the sphere of jurisdiction within which the law applies. This is a statement of principle, but to Suárez the principle must always be based upon the reason of things. In the present instance, he gives as the rational basis for the doctrine which he has laid down "that under the conditions specified the penalty is not imposed outside the state, but within the same." This can hardly be denied; but it was the custom of Suárez to probe deep and he therefore further develops the reason behind the principle. "It is," he continues, "assumed that this punishment must be imposed by human agency." To this assumption there can hardly be a dissent, since it is not within the province of human lawmakers to provide for spiritual punishments. Now "judges do not inflict

[1] II. i. 20.

punishment," he adds, "or exercise power upon persons who are dwelling abroad, but only upon those who return to the country." [1]

But what of the Papal decision, which Suárez has examined and explained, and which, in effect, declares that a law promulgated within a territory may be disobeyed with impunity outside of that territory? Does this decision conflict with the view just set forth? Suárez meets this question by reiterating that the meaning of the decision was merely that a law containing a penalty could not be operative outside of the jurisdiction of the lawmaker and hence, if a subject outside of that jurisdiction committed an offense against the law, he could not be considered guilty under the law as long as he remained outside of the jurisdiction in question. This is quite a different situation from that involved in the return of the offending subject, in which case, Suárez concludes that a penalty may properly become operative upon such return.

We should, however, have the exact language of Suárez on a matter of such importance—the "difference [is] between a law imposing a punishment *ipso facto*, and a law merely declaring a punishment that is to be imposed"; or, to carry the distinction further, as Suárez adds: "the first kind of law of itself inflicts a penalty and thus necessarily extends its binding character and power of execution outside its own territory." Such an extension would be unreasonable because the only way by which punishment under such a law could be inflicted was "by obliging the guilty person to execute the penalty upon himself," which, as Suárez points out, "is impossible." And it is not only impossible, but it is illogical, as he immediately demonstrates, "for if [the law in question] cannot compel one to, or restrain one from an action, much less will it be able to compel one to the execution of the penalty."

Now the situation is quite different as regards a law "which imposes a penalty that is to be inflicted by a judge," the reason being that such a law "is by the very nature of the case, a statute binding the judge to act in accordance with it, rather than a statute binding upon the criminal; and the judge dwells within the territorial limits of the state"—and these territorial limits are likewise the limits of his jurisdiction. Here Suárez has reached the heart of the matter and a final and utterly convincing argument on the territoriality of crime. For it would indeed be a curious state of affairs and a lamentable confusion of jurisdiction if judges were able to follow offenders and try offenses wherever committed.

It was the practice of the schoolmen, as it must be of every logical and successful disputant, not merely to meet the objections which had already been advanced but to foresee and overturn those which might have been or might be advanced. Therefore Suárez in the present instance overcomes an imaginary opponent and in so doing saves himself from a possible later attack by one less imaginary. The manner in which he handles the sup-

---

[1] For an application of this principle to a case of our day, see the leading case of *The Trial of Earl Russell* (before the King in Parliament), L. R. (1901) App. Cas. 446.

posed opponent is so perfect an example of the logical method of Suárez that it must be given in his own words:

The objection may be raised that the [guilty] subject is also bound in conscience to submit to the punishment in question. Our reply is that the said subject, strictly speaking, is not bound by this law until after sentence has been passed, when he is assumed to be already within the limits of the state.

An exterritorial crime, to be punishable within the state of the person committing it, must be a crime not only according to a law but a crime intrinsically—or as Suárez says, "essentially"—evil in itself; or it must be sufficiently forbidden in some other way than by the law of the prince imposing the penalty. For this law, as already pointed out, "can not itself prohibit the deed, outside of the limits of the state"; and the result of this is that the law in question "cannot designate any penalty" for the offense, "unless the deed is for some other reason assumed to be evil or sufficiently prohibited." There is an age-old example which may illustrate the doctrine of Suárez, although he himself does not employ it. It is none other than piracy under the law of nations, which is a law not merely for the international community, as such, but for each and every nation or state. Now as the jurisdiction of any nation, within the limits of international law, is universally admitted upon the high seas, and as piracy is prohibited under the law of nations, it may be punished by any nation as a violation of its own law, and the penalty of death inflicted under the law international. Thus piracy meets precisely the conditions which Suárez has laid down, for it is evil in itself, irrespective of the law of any one country; and not only is it evil in itself, but it is, in Suárez' very words, in "some other way sufficiently forbidden"—that is, by the law of nations.

In dealing with the exterritoriality of crime, Suárez—and perhaps the reader—has for the moment lost sight of the topic of his narrative, so to speak, namely, the subject living outside the territorial limits of the state, as described in the third of the categories with which he began the present chapter. He now recurs to this temporary resident abroad and states that by "living outside the territorial limits of the state . . . he does not lose his status as a subject in the essential sense." There is, however, a temporary change in his status, "that is to say," in the words of Suárez, "he ceases to exercise it"—meaning his status as subject—"in relation to the laws of his country, since he is living beyond the range of their [normal] operation." Applying this principle to the doctrine which he has been discussing, Suárez declares that "outside the territory no one is bound when the agent"—in the sense of the person performing the act—"and the object acted upon, and the action itself, are entirely without the limits of the state"; but the case is different if one or the other of these elements of the situation is within the territory the state in question. The inference which Suárez draws is, in fact, that "if the agent is outside, while the object with respect to which he offends is inside," then "the obligatory force of the law may be applicable."

Here Suárez cites an authority in whom, as we have already noted, he felt no small confidence. It is none other than Covarruvias, to the effect that "a law is not binding outside the limits of the state, unless the subject-matter of the law has in view the welfare of that same state." Speaking in the first person, Suárez says: "In my opinion, this is the true doctrine."

But Suárez felt that a certain elucidation and a qualification of this "true doctrine" were necessary, and he therefore informs us that, "strictly speaking, the proposition in question is not limited by the said doctrine, since offenses contrary to a law of the sort under discussion should be considered as having been committed, not without, but within the territory [of the law-maker]." There are two legal conditions under which the act might be committed: in one case the law may be affirmative; in the other, negative. Let us suppose that a law directs that a certain act be performed within the state which Suárez has in mind. If the person to whom the law applies fails to act in compliance with the law, that is, fails to perform the act within the jurisdiction in question, then, even though he is outside that jurisdiction, the offense may be considered as occurring within the state, since it redounds to the injury of the state. What, on the other hand, of a law which prohibits some act; in other words, the negative law which Suárez has mentioned as the second of the legal conditions? If the prohibition is disregarded by a national of the state, even though he be living abroad, and an injury to the state results therefrom, then, in the opinion of Suárez, the offense is clearly consummated in that state. The example which he gives is perfect of its kind, and one for which professors of the criminal law have, if we may speak from our own experience, an especial weakness. Thus, "a person corporeally outside the limits of the state or kingdom would, if he shot an arrow and thus killed a man within those boundaries, be clearly held to have sinned in the territory of the said state," and having committed such an act he would not merely transgress the law but would incur "in consequence," Suárez continues, "a liability to the censure"—in the sense of penalty or punishment—"if the latter should be provided for by the law in question."

But what of the situation in regard to *enclaves*—to use a term of the law of nations—or, as Suárez says, "with respect to exempt localities when they are otherwise enclosed within a state"? Having in a previous work[1] dealt with the matter in some detail, Suárez here contents himself by stating "simply" that "the same assertion does indeed hold true with respect to localities of this kind"; and he adds that this is also the view of the canonists.

But notwithstanding the authority of this view, Suárez as usual decided to enforce his statement by an example. "The same view is supported," he says, "by the laws above cited, in so far as it may be inferred from them that a prelate can not exercise his jurisdiction within the exempt territory." This illustration he considers as applicable to every superior; for, as the

[1] *De Censuris* (Coimbra, 1603).

locality is withdrawn from the territory, so the jurisdiction over the locality is also withdrawn from the territory, unless there be special exceptions under the law.   And Suárez concludes by quoting once more the decision of the Pope with reference to the prince and his jurisdiction, that *he who declares a law may be disobeyed with impunity outside his own territory*.

In a later portion of the same book (chapter xxxiii of Book III of the *De Legibus*), Suárez considers a further phase of the binding force of law, and as we have already seen[1], he discerns, as he says, "three elements," which, in his opinion, "must be distinguished in every law."   The first of these is "its binding force with respect to the conscience."   This Suárez called, speaking in the first person, "its directive force".   The second element he termed "its coercive force," and this he defines as that force "by means of which one may be punished according to law"—which we would term a sanction, in the language of modern jurisprudence.   And the third element, a matter of form rather than of substance, is "the force by which a definite form is laid down for contracts and similar legal acts."   This is possibly less important than the two preceding elements; yet it is often vital to the enforceability of an act legal in substance, though, unless the condition is complied with, not legal in form.

The question which Suárez prefixed to this chapter, "whether the domestic laws of any domain are strictly binding upon aliens while they are living therein", he considers in relation to these three elements since, in his opinion, they give rise to "some peculiar difficulties".

On these matters there was a twofold divergence of opinion, but, after all, there was similarity if not identity in the basis of each of the views, namely, "that non-resident foreigners (*peregrini*) are not subjects."   The reason for this similarity?   "The status of subjects," he says, "in so far as moral direction and obligation are concerned, is to be acquired only through domicile, or at least through quasi-domicile."   This may be the legal point of view.   Nevertheless "the law of a locality," he adds, "is binding in conscience upon aliens and guests as long as they dwell therein," the reason being that residence confers jurisdiction, and so long as individuals reside in the locality in question, its laws create an obligation on the part of all residents to observe them.   The view of Suárez in favor of assuming jurisdiction over resident aliens and guests is that a law, to be law, must be of general application within the jurisdiction in which it is applied and therefore binding "for the period of their residence, on all persons actually living therein."

This may be admitted.   But what of transients?   It would seem that they should be included, for the purpose of jurisdiction, in the term "residents"; for they are actually within the community, even when in transit.

In behalf of the view which he had stated as a personal one, Suárez advances three proofs which make it of universal application.   The first of the three proofs is one of "the final cause."   Here Suárez considers what would

[1] *Supra*, p. 54.

be the result if the law were not applicable to the alien and native alike, stating that, if such inequality existed, "disputes and scandals would result." He thus reaches the conclusion, from his viewpoint of the "final cause", that "it is morally necessary for the good government of a province, locality or territory that the laws made for the same should have this [universally binding] effect; for it is necessary to the peace and good morals of that locality"—or, we may add, of any locality—"that aliens should conform to the customs of its people" as long as they live in the same jurisdiction.

Having stated the principle, Suárez indicates the authority, which is none other than the *Decretum*, and that greatest of teachers, "experience". And, as a schoolman, he concludes on the basis of these premises that "since laws are established with a view to the common welfare, peace and good morals of the country, it is necessary that they should possess the [universal] force in question."

After dealing thus with the final cause or purpose—or, as the Greeks put it, design in nature—Suárez passes to the second of his proofs, to be found in the "efficient cause", that is to say, the means or channel by which the purpose is carried out; in other words—and especially in our day—the legislative power.

Since the state, as Suárez has said more than once on the authority of no less a person than Aristotle, should be a perfect community, it rests with the chief executive, as we would say, or, as Suárez says, with the "civil governor . . . to preserve his state and to safeguard its morals," for which purpose the executive in question is presumed to have the necessary power; and, having this power, he exercises it in the making of laws "which are binding upon all living within his domain." "It is on this ground," Suárez continues, "that he is empowered to punish aliens who commit crimes" within his jurisdiction. But this is not enough for Suárez. By "aliens"—as he has been using the term—we would understand foreign persons actually resident within the domain. However, Suárez here enlarges his conception to include within the power of the civil governor the right "to bind by his laws all persons engaged in activities within his realm," provided, of course, that such compulsion on his part "is necessary to the welfare of that realm." In short, the law in question would apply not only to permanent alien residents within the country, but also to temporary residents and even to transients.

In the two preceding proofs, Suárez has considered the matter primarily from the point of view of the act of the state in which the aliens reside. Now he turns to the third proof, which pertains to foreigners within the state. "The same truth," he declares, "is evident from the standpoint of the aliens" and "there are grounds sufficient to justify their subjection to such an extent that they may be bound by the laws of the territory." Suárez does not mean that foreigners should be assimilated to natives nor, on the other hand, that they are to be discriminated against. The duration or

degree of subjection, in Suárez' opinion, is not determined by the length of stay in the country. On the contrary, the degree of subjection is the same regardless of the length of residence, "the sole requirement for that subjection being actual sojourn and presence, even though that sojourn may be of short duration."

There then follows a passage in which Suárez displays that keenness, that subtlety, that penetration of thought which characterizes him when at his best, and there can be no doubt that it is not merely the philosopher, or indeed the jurist, but also the *litterateur* as well as the logician who speaks: "For just as a man in changing his domicile from one place to another, by that very act manifests his will to be bound permanently by the laws of that new territory, or else become bound in consequence of his act and despite his will to the contrary; even so any person who wills to sojourn in a given locality for a brief time, by that very act manifests or should manifest a will to subject himself temporarily to the government of that territory in everything relating to general customs and laws." So much for the *litterateur*. Now for the logician: "This statement is confirmed by reversing the argument. For an inhabitant of any territory, withdrawing from it for a brief period, at once and throughout that period ceases to be bound by the laws thereof, according to the argument of the preceding chapter; and, consequently, during that time, he is not actually a subject. Hence the converse will also hold true; for the principle is the same, and equity demands that in both cases equality—that is to say, due proportion"—the Greek wins over the Latin—"shall be observed."

Here Suárez pauses to consider the question of "scandal" in its relation to the obligation of the alien. He was of the opinion that the mere desire to avoid scandal was not the true basis of the obligation, although granting that it "accidentally increases the obligation." What, then, is its real relationship to the obligation? "At the most an occasion or motive," Suárez answers, "which impels the legislator to make the law." But suppose this occasion or motive has lapsed. Does the obligation survive? Yes; because the obligation is not due to scandal: the obligation is due to the law, and therefore, as long as the law exists, the obligation exists, "just as," Suárez says, "the carrying of arms is forbidden, to prevent quarrels, and women are forbidden to adorn themselves in one way or another,"—we quote Suárez as a good churchman, giving his exact words in order on this occasion to disassociate ourselves from his personal opinion—"to avoid scandal." But, as he said above, "the obligation to abstain from these acts exists," not because of the scandal, but "*per se*, by reason of the laws themselves." Of course, in this connection, strangers are bound to conform to the same extent as the subjects, "not only for the sake of avoiding scandal, but also because of the law itself and because they are under a sufficient obligation to obedience, as has been explained." Here we have again a cleancut expression of the opinion of Suárez that residence is a fundamental element of jurisdiction.

This does not mean, however, that aliens should be in all respects subject to the same law as are the residents of the country in which they may happen to sojourn.   They should, however, be subject to law, and it is the province and the right of the lawmaking power of the country to determine the content and application of the law affecting them.   In the opinion of Suárez, non-residents might have a "peculiar mode of living", or be "located in a given place" and therefore "in many matters, they may require separate statutes."   To this extent they are, he says again, subjects, "by the mere fact of their sojourn."   There is, however, a twofold requirement: that the special laws applicable to foreigners "be just and expedient, not only to the locality in question, but also to the non-residents themselves," observing, as Suárez discriminatingly says, "a due proportion between the two," in order that they may thus "satisfy every qualification for placing the non-residents under a valid obligation."

Turning now to the coercive element of law, Suárez maintains that it applies not merely to natives and to foreigners who may be domiciled in the country, but to temporary residents, or even to transients.   For a transgression of a law of the country renders persons of each and all of these classes equally liable to punishment, "either through a judge or through the force of the law itself, if it involves a penalty *ipso facto*."

Why does Suárez, it may be asked, mention specifically a penalty *ipso facto*?   Because in his opinion, and he so says, the "directive power would not be efficacious unless coercive power were annexed thereto."   Furthermore, the alien is bound not only in conscience, but in law, to obedience, and this being the case, in transgressing law, "he commits an offence" both in the territory and against the state, and in consequence, "by reason of this offence also he remains subject to the coercive power of the commonwealth in question."   This rule was subject, however, to one limitation, that "the non-resident foreigner shall not be superior in rank to the author of the law in question," that is, the sovereign power of the state, "since no superior can be subjected to an inferior by coercive authority."   Nor, it may be added, in our own behalf, may sovereigns equal in authority, or their representatives, be subjected one to the other, since the inequality of superior to inferior is lacking.

This means that a sovereign, or his official representative (that is, ambassador) coming within the jurisdiction in question is not subject to the laws, because being equal, he is not inferior, and, according to the conception which Suárez upholds, it is only the inferior who is obliged to yield to coercive authority.   This, it may be stated in passing, is international law as approved by the centuries.

It may also be said in passing, without dwelling upon what is self-evident, that a statute may be enacted to punish offenses which, as Suárez says, "may be committed in the future."   Such is the case with most laws; indeed they should not be retroactive.

Suárez now proceeds to discuss the third of the three elements with which he began this chapter, that of form, giving concrete examples, such as a will or a contract made within a given territory which, as he had previously said, without pausing to give examples, should follow the laws of the realm in all such matters.   The will or the contract of an alien subject would clearly be void, Suárez says—and it should be void—if not made in the form prescribed by the laws of the land.   The reason for this is the universality of law within the jurisdiction to which it applies for, if it were not universally applicable, it would cease, in so far as the exception is concerned, to be a law, the alien being to that extent privileged, and, according to Suárez, the alien is not accorded a privilege any more than is the native inhabitant.   Therefore the law of the country "obliges all persons in that locality to observe also the form of procedure which it prescribes; and, just as it includes the power to punish, so also it includes the power to invalidate."

Suárez had previously cited a will of an alien by way of example.   He now proceeds to the question of taxes as a further illustration; for is anything—in the words of our Franklin—more certain than death and taxes?   Not inappropriately, therefore, Suárez asks "whether a foreigner is bound to pay them"—meaning taxes.   Fortunately for us citizens, he confines his attention to "a foreigner," and answers his own question in the affirmative.   If the alien owns property within a given country, upon which, according to the laws obtaining in that country, a tax is due; or, as Suárez adds, if he performs any act in that place which is subject to tax by the laws of the country, "then there will be an obligation to pay that tax, . . . generally speaking, and"—a proviso which we would expect in all of the principles which Suárez lays down—"assuming that the tax is a just one."   The case is otherwise with regard to those taxes "which are of a personal nature."   Thus, to give a further example, which Suárez no doubt had in mind but which he did not himself cite, a foreigner temporarily resident in a given locality, would not be subject to a poll tax, although if during his sojourn he purchased a house or lands, or entered into a transaction subject to the internal revenue laws of the realm, he would be subject to taxes in the same manner as in the case of natives of the country.

There are many and interesting examples which could be cited in addition to those which Suárez has given; and although they were sufficient for his purpose, a few others which are of interest in our day and in our country are mentioned to show that Suárez did not write for his day but for all time, just as he wrote not for his own country but for all countries.

Let us take the case of foreigners who come to our shores but who, by the laws of the United States, can not themselves become naturalized citizens.[1] We shall also suppose that they have a child born after their arrival.   That

---

[1] Act of May 6, 1882 [22 Stat. 61 (1882), 8 U. S. Code, § 363 (1926)]:
"That hereafter no State court or court of the United States shall admit Chinese to citizenship; and all laws in conflict with this act are hereby repealed."

child is, by virtue of the Fourteenth Amendment to the Constitution,[1] an American citizen because the child is born within and subject to the jurisdiction of the United States. Such also is the nationality of a child born in American jurisdiction of foreign parents in transit through the United States. In both these cases the laws of the country apply to the foreigner as to the native, in that their children are American citizens if born within the United States. This is citizenship *ex jure soli.* As a result of the law, in many foreign countries, where nationality depends upon *jus sanguinis,* the child born in the United States of foreign parents might have a double nationality. Thus under the law of countries adopting the test of blood relationship, the child in question would have not only American nationality but the nationality of his parents as well.

It is pertinent to reconsider for a moment the view of Victoria, who held that a child should and could have only the nationality of the place of birth;[2] for does he not say explicitly that the child in question has the nationality of the country in which he is born, and, if he did not have this nationality, he would be stateless, because he could not have the nationality of a country in which he was not born? This view, it may be said in passing, has two great virtues. It gives every human being a single nationality, and leaves no human being without a nationality.

We have ourselves instanced on a previous page[3] the exemption of a sovereign from the laws of a foreign country within whose jurisdiction he may happen to be, as an illustration of the rule that a law, to be binding, must be the law of a superior. It is therefore a consequence of the immunity of the sovereign from the laws of the country in which he happens to sojourn that in the case of a child born to an ambassador or minister or diplomatic agent (to use an all-inclusive term)—who is, as the agent of the foreign sovereign power, exempt from the jurisdiction of the country to which he is accredited or through which he happens to pass—such a child is born a citizen or subject of the country of the ambassador, minister, or diplomatic agent in question.

* * *

Custom played a large part in the growth of law, and indeed it was and continues to be the source of much of the law, especially in the case of the

---

[1] "Sec. 1. All persons born or naturalized in the United States, and subject to the jurisdiction thereof, are citizens of the United States and of the State wherein they reside. No State shall make or enforce any law which shall abridge the privileges or immunities of citizens of the United States; nor shall any State deprive any person of life, liberty, or property, without due process of law; nor deny to any person within its jurisdiction the equal protection of the laws."

[2] See Victoria's *De Indis,* Section III, no. 5, Carnegie Institution edition above cited, pp. 153-4: "If children of any Spaniard be born there and they wish to acquire citizenship, it seems they can not be barred either from citizenship or from the advantages enjoyed by other citizens—I refer to the case where the parents had their domicile there. The proof of this is furnished by the rule of the law of nations, that he is to be called and is a citizen who is born within the state (*Code,* VII. lxii. 11). And the confirmation lies in the fact that, as man is a civil animal, whoever is born in any one state is not a citizen of another state. Therefore, if he were not a citizen of the state referred to, he would not be a citizen of any state, to the prejudice of his rights under both natural law and the law of nations."

[3] *Supra* p. 109.

law of nations.   It is not surprising, therefore, that Suárez devoted an entire book (the seventh of his *De Legibus*) to Custom, its origin, its nature and its effects.

Custom, Suárez says, both preceded and followed law.   It preceded it inevitably because custom is the unwritten law and custom antedated writing; and it followed law because custom is ever with us.   Speaking of "law" in a formal sense, Suárez says, "it is certain . . . that the written is the principal form of law," and he adds that from it "custom derives in great measure its strength and meaning."   In custom three terms are first to be noted: *usus, mos, consuetudo*, which are "closely kindred in meaning" and the result of "free—that is, properly human—action."   The word "free" is of no small importance, because it implies voluntary action, and without voluntary action custom, as such, can not arise, as Suárez demonstrates more fully in a later passage.

As three terms are used, there must be a difference between them, however closely they may be allied.   Thus *usus* (and indeed so it is with the English equivalent) applies "equally to a general habit of action and to single actions"; but the term "*mos* . . . may not properly be applied to a single action as *usus* may be, but only to a repetition of like actions."   Differing in definition, they are, however, "practically the same" in their relation to the general subject of custom, St. Thomas ascribing to both the same meaning— "the repetition of a voluntary action."   Custom is a thing of two elements, Suárez says: one being "formal custom," a "series of repeated actions," identical with "usage" in that both are voluntary and matter of fact; the second element is the "after effect of repeated acts."   In a merely material sense, the distinction is more apparent than real, inasmuch as each element is, after all, a matter of fact.   Therefore Suárez passes to the spiritual conception inherent in another phase of the second element of custom.   His exact language is—"a second after effect is one of the moral order, a faculty compelling the performance of a certain action or nullifying another obligation."   This he calls "customary law or a legal rule introduced by custom."   But it is not every custom which creates "a legal rule," in confirmation of which he immediately adds that "an evil custom . . . creates no legal force; nor does one that grows out of the observance of a law—although it is spoken of as custom."   For, in truth, what is implicit in a law is part of the law and therefore not custom.   Therefore, "to limit our definition," continues Suárez, "to that custom of fact which is capable of introducing law, we must include in it . . . the note that the custom is an authorized repetition of actions that contravene no established law."   Thus the custom of fact, which in the usual course of events can introduce law, must not be in opposition to the laws already in existence; for the custom which Suárez has at present in mind is only, as we have seen, that "authorized repetition of actions that contravene no established law"; or again, it must be custom "in which all the conditions required by the law are fulfilled."

There are exceptions, of course, to this statement, and these, as we shall see, Suárez takes up in subsequent pages. While custom is a thing of practice, there is practice and practice. There must be "public practice" of the community, in order that custom may generate law and its strict obligation. Therefore the converse is true. "Private practice of a person," or indeed "of a family," is not sufficient to establish a "legal rule." In a word, the custom which "suffices to introduce law must be drawn from the general practice of the people," that is, of "the community as a whole"; or, as in the case of the law of nations and the international community, "of all, or the greater part of its members." That is to say, custom is the generator of law; and in the sense in which the term customary law is used by Suárez, it is popular law as distinct from legislative law. In the Anglo-Saxon system, it becomes "common law."

Suárez has before defined the term *jus*, but in connection with custom, he finds it necessary to consider this term afresh. Therefore he says that it "has two meanings", the one signifying "the faculty of use," that is to say, "ownership or quasi-ownership"; while in the second sense *jus* is defined by Suárez as "a right that carries the power to bind and command: . . . the right of law or legal right."

Suárez observes that in his two definitions of *jus* lies the distinction between "prescription" and "custom" in the legal sense; for prescription may arise from private use by an individual and therefore is not general custom, which arises only from public use; hence prescription can not generate law but can only confer a right of ownership—in other words, *jus* in the sense first defined by Suárez. Instead of introducing a legal rule, "prescription" confers rather "a right of ownership or one of a similar kind"; and he renders the definition more explicit by examples such as "the use or enjoyment of some material thing, as a house, an article of clothing; or, of an immaterial thing, as, the exercise of jurisdiction or the right of suffrage." The contrast is further brought out by Suárez' statement that "a custom of the people is essential for the kind of *jus* which is law"; whereas, in general, "usage of a private person is sufficient for prescription," although the community "as a moral person" may at times exercise in its own behalf a prescriptive right.

Further illustrating the distinction between custom and prescription Suárez says that "for the validity of a true, legal custom . . . the consent of the community, or of the sovereign against whom the prescription is in a certain sense obtained is necessary." The consent of the community is unnecessary, however, in the case of prescription against a private person, that is, prescription in the ordinary sense of the term. In the first instance, Suárez is speaking of prescription against the community or against its sovereign by the community, which is not prescription in the usual legal meaning of the term; in the second case he is referring to prescription, as such, that is, against private individuals, in which case consent is not necessary, and here again Suárez proves himself to be a lawyer as well as a theo-

logian.   The prescription against the community—that is to say, against the sovereign authority of the community—establishes custom if the community consents to it; the prescription against a private individual does not. In custom, as in prescription, time is an element, but it differs in duration. The length of time for prescription, Suárez says, "is fixed by law."   On the other hand, there is no time limit in the matter of custom; "rather," says Suárez, "that period suffices which gives time for manifesting the consent of the sovereign or of the people."

In the conclusion stated in the third chapter of Book VII, Suárez, for the benefit of lawyer as well as layman, distinguishes the various kinds of custom in the legal sense, saying that from the "variety of custom arises a variety and multiplicity in customary law."   We shall group the varieties in numbered paragraphs.

1. "If the community is ecclesiastical its custom will introduce ecclesiastical law."   But suppose that, in the words of Suárez, "the custom be that of the whole Church."   The result will be the creation of "a general rule of canon law concerning which"—as he well knew—"there are many decrees." If the custom were that of a whole ecclesiastical province, there would result what might be termed a national ecclesiastical law of custom; while if the custom were that of a particular bishopric, "then the law" would be, so to speak, "synodal or diocesan"; should it be "of a private chapter or community, the law will be, as it were, municipal."

Thus for Suárez the theologian.   Now for Suárez the lawyer:

2. "The same sort of relation will hold true," he continues, "of the civil customs."   Thus it is that, "if the custom be that of one kingdom, it will be, so to speak, that of the realm," and may introduce a civil law applicable to the entire country.   If, again, the custom applies to one province, but not to others, it may bring into being what we might call a "provincial" law, or, if we are to speak of still narrower limits, those of the city or town, then the custom arising within such a municipality may introduce municipal law.

Now for the third category of legal custom, that giving rise to—

3. "General civil law," that is to say, law arising from similar customs in different countries, with the result that these laws, in howsoever many different jurisdictions they may apply, are the same.   It is such a general civil law which was often termed the *jus gentium*, meaning not laws between the states but similar laws within the states; "and," observes Suárez, "even though their laws are sometimes alike in respect of a certain custom, they observe not one, but many customs which are like one another; just as in various kingdoms there will be many laws that are alike, but the law of one is not binding on the subjects of any other."

This category of customs arises within different communities and relates to matters of national concern.   And however numerous these different communities with identical customs may be, the customs are not, in the

international sense, universal since they deal with internal and not international matters; for if they were international, they would be, in the conception of Suárez, a part of the law of nations, which, in Suárez' day and in our own, was custom not within nations but between nations.

Having distinguished custom of fact from custom of law and having also distinguished the varieties of customary law arising within a country, Suárez now makes what he terms "a third principal division of custom," and under the first head is "that which is according to law"; the second, that which is "beyond the ambit of the existing law"; and the third, "that counter to law". This threefold division applies to custom in relation to the three branches of law, to "the natural law, to positive divine law, and to human law."

Let us confine our attention for the moment to the application of these three divisions of custom to the natural law. On this point Suárez says positively that "no custom . . . can exist outside of the ambit of that law." A particular custom may, of course, be spoken of as being "in accord with the natural law, since it proceeds from it, and through it the natural law is observed," but since custom can not exist outside of natural law and usage, a usage which is contrary to that law and violates it is not, in the words of Suárez, "worthy of the name of custom." Indeed, he says, in no uncertain terms, "it rather merits that given it in the language of the laws—corruption." Hence such a so-called custom can "have no effect on law, either by abrogating or introducing it"—and this on no less an authority than St. Thomas Aquinas—"since the law of nature is, as we have seen, immutable and so cannot be abrogated."

There is another kind of custom which may in a sense be outside the natural law, in that it consists, as Suárez points out, of "actions that are, according to a probable opinion, indifferent" to the law natural; or it may consist of "good actions, which although they are approved by the natural law or enjoined by it as to mode or manner . . . are not absolutely enjoined as to performance." In this sense, custom is related not to the mandatory or prohibitory phases of natural law but to its concessive phase.

What, we may now ask, is the relation of custom to the law of nations? It may be in conformity therewith, but in such a case it is "an extension of universal custom and is consequently the same law and not a new one." But may a custom be contrary to the *jus gentium*? This is quite another matter. Certain jurists held that such a custom could not "introduce law". But to Suárez the matter was but one of terminology; if the term *jus gentium* was used in the sense of international law, there was no difficulty. "I believe, therefore," he says in the first person, "it must be agreed that it is not absolutely inconceivable that a part of the law of nations should be cancelled by custom." The reason was that the law of nations, although related to the natural law, was not natural law and therefore that what is "contrary" merely to the law of nations, as such, is not intrinsically wrong

as would be the case were it contrary to natural law.   A familiar example here meets us, that "respecting the slavery of prisoners captured in war." This was a practice introduced by the *jus gentium* but one which, Suárez says "may be"—we are glad to add "is"—"abolished by custom."   But such abrogation by custom can apply only to part of the law of nations, because "it is morally impossible that the whole of this law could be abolished."   Why?   To bring about a total abolition all nations would need to concur in "a custom contrary to the *jus gentium*"—meaning the law of nations in its entirety.   But indeed, as Suárez points out, "such uniformity in any matter is rarely attained," and in the matter in hand there is an additional and special reason why uniformity would be rare, in that the *jus gentium* is in close harmony with nature.   Man, we may observe, rarely departs from nature, and then only at his peril.

This does not mean, however, that an individual nation may not under special circumstances adopt "a custom contrary to the *jus gentium*."   In such a case, the citizens or subjects of the nation in question would be bound by the custom; but the custom may not prejudice the rights of any other nation or the rights of its subjects, for while a nation can renounce the exercise of a right for itself or for its people it may not renounce the right in behalf of another nation.

Suárez reinforces his opinion on this point by an example as up to date today as it was in his—the use of highways.   "If," he says, "in some territory passage over highways were permitted only upon irksome conditions, such a custom could not extend to foreigners who allow such passage without such conditions."   This is not only a matter of equal treatment but of reciprocity.   There are, we may add, certain minor restrictions of traffic which would not constitute "the irksome conditions" of Suárez.   Thus, the American motorist on the English highways will find that the customary traffic rules of the country require him to keep to the left instead of to the right.   This requirement may sometimes be "irksome" to him personally— accustomed as he is to the American rule, "keep to the right"—but it is not in violation of the law of nations.   However, if the cause for a restriction of this nature should cease to exist, it is the view of Suárez that the restriction itself would then be unjust, for it would be "contrary to the natural law to extend such a custom to foreigners."

Suárez, trained as a schoolman, had what we must call an ingrained habit of meeting and forestalling objections to any and every solution; and it is permissible to say that many a modern solution could not withstand this test of the schoolman's logic.   It was generally admitted, according to Suárez, that a "prince may not exact anything contrary to the *jus gentium*, because his jurisdiction is inferior thereto," and it might therefore be argued, "neither can the custom of one nation derogate from the *jus gentium*, because the custom is no more powerful than the law of one sovereign."   But Suárez is ready with a reply.   What the prince might not do alone, the prince, with

that most fundamental of elements of Suárez' society—the consent of the people—might do; and indeed Suárez is of opinion that, even without the consent of the prince, the community might establish a rule contrary to the *jus gentium* "by common consent and custom." This is a matter of such importance that it is well to examine closely what Suárez has in mind. He is not dealing with an untrammelled right of nations to unmake the law of nations at their will. What he does have in mind is relief from the application of a certain rule of the law of nations which might be unsuitable under conditions peculiar to a particular country. Thus, speaking of the ruler as a prince—and meaning thereby a prince who governs his country for its own good—he says: "I maintain that a prince may, perhaps, enact a law contrary to the *jus gentium* by departing therefrom in the non-observance of some rule which is deemed inexpedient in his territories and for his subjects." Now for his example, which makes clear the conception of Suárez. "For example," he continues, "he"—meaning the prince—"might enact not a law against slavery, but one that all men should be free, or something similar." It should be added that under the law of nations of Suárez' day, slavery was still permitted; therefore a ruler might not enact a law directly abolishing it; or, as Chief Justice Marshall said in the *Antelope* case,[1] no single nation may make a law of nations. The most that the prince could do would be to derogate from the law of nations by the passage of a law applicable only within his domain and to his own subjects, that "all men should be free"—an act on his part not in opposition to natural reason or the proper government of the state. For it is by these two factors that the propriety of such a law must invariably be tested.

This is but an incident by way of illustration. The right of the prince is not limited to this example for just as he might enact a law contrary to a municipal custom of his realms, so also he may, Suárez says, "make a rule contrary to that portion of the *jus gentium* which affects his government." The reason? The law of nations is, by "its universality alone," not "the stronger or more immutable with respect to his subjects; it is only so with respect to [his relations with] other nations."

The right to hold slaves was, in Suárez' day, a universal right, but the prince had the power to renounce it on behalf of his subjects. Fortunately all civilized nations have today seen fit to take the same action.

The people of a state may renounce a right which it possesses under the law of nations, but they can not renounce a right of other nations, because such renunciation is and must always depend upon the consent of the people to whom the right belongs.

"Custom of fact" is a series of actions as distinct from a rule which may arise from a series of actions: the one being a matter of fact; the other a matter of law. Thus Suárez looks upon custom of fact as "a form of observance of a pre-existing law." The repetition of actions (which is called

[1] 10 Wheat. 66 (1825).

"custom of fact") should be in conformity with the law, as otherwise it would constitute a series of illegal actions; and therefore, in the main, custom is conformity with law already in existence.   It is not however, a direct observance of the law in the sense that the actions are required merely with a view to complying with the law.   Nevertheless they are, as Suárez says, a form of observance, in that they comply with, and are not contrary to, the law already in existence.

In a word, in Suárez' conception, custom of fact as distinct from custom which has become law is to be looked upon not as making but as evidence of the law; and in behalf of Suárez, a statute of the Permanent Court of International Justice[1] may be invoked, prescribing among the principles which the court shall apply "international custom, as evidence of a general practice accepted as law."   Custom as thus conceived is a matter of evidence, rather than of the introduction of law; or, stated in still another way: it is the fulfilment and not the creation of law.   "Wherefore," continues Suárez, "Baldus . . . truly says that a custom in harmony with law is not regulative in character but one which is imitative of the law, or, as it were executive."

What happens to custom, however, if the law of which the custom of fact is evidence should be abrogated by another law?   Suárez replies on the authority of the Gloss[2] and of Panormitanus[3] that the custom which grew out of the observance of the law is then "abolished also, even if no mention is made of it."   This could only be so if the custom is looked upon as a part of the law.   If the case were otherwise, the custom would be independent of the law and therefore would continue to exist notwithstanding the abrogation of the law.   Indeed, custom of fact may be said to confirm the law, or, as the statute of the Permanent Court of International Justice puts it, it may be "evidence of the law".[4]   Or as Gratian,[5] the authority upon which Suárez relies, held: "Laws are established when they are promulgated; confirmed when they are approved by the practice [mores] of those who use them",—a matter which Bartolus[6] explains by saying that "such custom confirms the law not directly, but by holding back or prohibiting . . . the opposite custom and the abrogation of the law."   And as Suárez puts it, "this sort of custom"—meaning custom of fact—"may be said to bear aid to the law . . . since the custom makes easier the observance of the law, and, in a certain sense, [the law itself] less liable to change."   There is thus a protective function of custom of fact in its relation to law.

But, in addition, custom may be said "to interpret the law, indeed it is called in the law *an excellent interpreter of the law.*"   The reason?   Because "it"—custom—"indicates in what sense the law was originally made and received."

---

[1] Statute of the Permanent Court of International Justice, Article 38, § 2.
[2] On *Sext.* I. iv. 1.   [3] On *Decretals*, I, iv. 11, n. 21.
[4] Statute, *ibid.*   [5] *Decretum*, I. iv. 3.   [6] On *Digest*, I. iii. 32, n. 4.

Those who have read, and especially pondered, Suárez, have a suspicion that there is no limit to the depth and subtlety of his exposition; but a merciful man at heart, he relieves our apprehensions by coming to a "finally" in his discussion "of another effect" of custom of fact, namely, "the extension of law"; and the illustration he takes is of his calling: that "a law may be made originally for laymen only" but that, as a result of custom, "clerics" follow it and it becomes a law for them as for laymen.

Turning now to custom according to law, Suárez points out that it may be defined in two senses: first in the sense that it "exists by force of law and by its command;" and secondly, "in the sense that it is modelled on the law, in its likeness, that it imitates it." Although both senses relate to custom according to law, it is the first of these conceptions of custom with which Suárez wishes at present to deal. Recurring to the matter of interpretation, which he had already mentioned, Suárez continues that "such custom does not really extend law except by way of the interpretation that it may give to the words of the law." And he draws a distinction, saying that in the example of the clerics above given the custom is not according to the law, in the interpretive sense. Why? Because "it does not proceed from the civil law, but from the free will of those who wished to perform what the civil law prescribed, even if they are not bound thereby."

Another "finally"—in this case a "lastly". Suárez divides custom "into positive and privative or negative custom." Now "positive usage" is the origin of the former, consisting, to the extent that it is custom of fact, "in a certain repetition of actions," but, in so far as it is custom of law, "it sets up an inclination and an obligation to act," whereas a "negative custom" is negative in the sense that it is passive in character, originating "from non-usage"; but "to the extent that this non-usage is frequent and continuous," it assumes the characteristics of custom, being indeed "of a quasi-positive nature"; and to this extent it approaches the custom of law, for where "it establishes some legal rule," it fosters, as in the case of the positive custom, "an inclination and obligation to refrain from action."

But whatever form custom may assume—chameleon-like though it seems betimes to be—it must always possess as a constant element, a moral character. For as law can not truly be said to exist unless it be moral, so custom of any kind or variety can not establish a legal obligation unless it be a moral custom.

From the beginning, the conception of the Spanish School was that of the morality of law, and therefore the custom with which its members dealt could not be immoral—or indeed unmoral—for morality, in their conception, was the essence of good law whether natural, statutory, or customary.

Suárez having hitherto dealt in some detail with the effect of custom upon law, now turns to the opposite phase of the matter, as it were,—the effect of law upon custom, and the first of these effects is the annulment of custom by law in one way or another. Of these ways there are no less than three, and

Suárez ventures to add a fourth.   First there is abrogation of custom by law; then prohibition of custom by law; third, condemnation of custom; and the fourth, which he has attempted to add—and which, as a matter of fact, he does add—is "an unqualified opposition to custom."

First of abrogation, which is not necessarily "equivalent to a condemnation" of custom, because the abrogation may occur, not because the custom is of an unreasonable nature but merely because "it pleases the lawmaker" to abrogate the custom, on the ground that this course is the "more expedient" under existing conditions.   Law should look to the greater rather than to the lesser expedient.

In the case of prohibition, not merely the existing custom but that which "is to be established," is prohibited; in other words, the law not merely prohibits the present custom but checks its introduction in the future.

Now for condemnation, which the law may accomplish in either of two ways: "by a purely declaratory law; and by a law passed to quiet a doubt." If the custom is condemned by a declaratory law, it would be on the ground that the custom is obviously so "base as to be contrary to natural or divine law"; or else because it is not merely "useless" but "harmful to general welfare."   Let us suppose, however, that it is not clearly evident whether the custom is good or bad.   In this case, the law which condemns it will, as Suárez states, "quiet a doubt."   Such a condemnation is "unquestionably" within the province of human law and "especially" of the canon law; and may be in the highest degree proper in the interest of good morals.

The fourth of the ways in which law may affect custom Suárez has previously referred to as "opposition"; but he now uses a different term for the sake of precision, namely, "interruption."   How can this be brought about? The interruption of a custom can only be "by the whole community in which the custom has been followed".   Such a view is in conformity with the doctrine of government by majority, for which Suárez firmly stands. "For," he says, "the acts of a few private individuals do not annul the consent of the community," and therefore they "can not destroy a general custom."   If, however, the community has delegated power to a chief executive (whether prince or president), then the interruption—or, to use another term employed by Suárez, "suppression"—of the custom might be brought about through "the public authority of the one holding the necessary power," not necessarily by a direct abolition of the custom but by decreeing a public punishment for an individual who had observed the custom, thus indicating that the custom, in the language of Suárez, "was not in accord with the will of the Prince."

These matters were, in a way, preliminary to the more profound examination of custom which we would expect from Suárez; and with the preliminaries out of the way, he is now ready to consider "the matter and form in the constitution of a custom."   As regards the former—meaning the matter —he finds that custom and human law are similar, if not identical: "in so far

as the custom is a juridical entity its matter is the same as that of written human law." The difference between them is rather one of form, or, in Suárez' words, "in the mode of expression through which they exist."

As a result of the labor of lawmakers throughout the centuries, certain definite prerequisites of form and expression have come into use for written statutes, but, as Suárez points out, "in the law of custom, there is no special form, sensible and external." There is indeed nothing except those actions which constitute custom, and these, continues Suárez, "in so far as they are tokens of consent, may be called the unwritten words by which this kind of law is engraved upon the memory of men."

There is an additional distinction which arises in the comparison between custom and written law. The statute does not go into effect until it is promulgated. Not so with the custom, for which "no promulgation is required"; and the reason for this is stated with maximlike brevity—"custom, through the usage itself, is its own public manifestation and promulgation."

Suárez now turns to another phase of the relation between custom and law: what is the result if a private custom is in conflict with a general law? This brings us again to the question of prescription; for, as Suárez points out, an exemption from the obligation of the law might result from obtaining a prescriptive right through custom, since the acquisition of this right "may change the matter" of the law and thus "terminate the obligation of that law." To illustrate this, Suárez refers to the fact that "a private custom can exempt, or rather remove the obligation of the law from, a certain person." Here, however, what happens is not a "derogation from the general law, but an abolition of its subject-matter"; and a change of subject-matter as a result of change of circumstances, as Suárez had already pointed out, and as he here reiterates, may even affect the natural law. From which fact the principle which he has just stated gained, he felt, a notable support.

So much for private custom and its effect on law through prescription. But may such a custom have a direct effect on law, or, in the words of Suárez, may it "derogate from the general law by abating its obligation directly and of its own force"? The answer to this question is an unequivocal denial, stated in the first person. "This we maintain is impossible." Why? "Because a private custom of breaking the law never excuses the fault; on the contrary, it rather increases it."

This does not mean, however, that law can not be changed by a group of individuals, although it does mean that individuals acting alone can not change the law. Not every group of individuals, however, has the power in question. Thus a legal custom, in Suárez' language, can not be "introduced by any community whatever, but only by one possessing the capacity for legislative authority over itself; or, at least, by a community of sufficient perfection to be the subject of the law properly so-called."

What is this community? The *civitas*, or *state*. The reason for this limitation on the introduction of legal custom is, in simplest terms, that law derives its consent from the community, the general rule in such a matter being that only the majority, not the minority—much less the individual—can act for the people, whether in the making of law or in the formation of custom or the unmaking of either; because, as we have ourselves said, custom is popular law. In the words of Suárez, "the consent, therefore, of the majority of the community is also to be held as that of the whole community, and sufficient, consequently, for the establishment of custom."

In this case, it is sufficient that the custom be of itself a public one; and in the case of custom, as of other law, ignorance is no excuse, provided that knowledge may be had, and is had, by the majority. How is the majority, or the major portion, to be computed? Fortunately Suárez found that there was "a general agreement on this point", the majority or major portion consisting "only" of "such persons as can give consent to a legal custom." This excludes infants and all mentally defective persons. Suárez, celebrated as he was and living in the world but, as it were, not a part of it, curiously had observed that this perfect community consisted not merely of men but of men and women. He was aware, as are we of what is termed a more "modern" age, that "some would also exclude women entirely, on the ground that they can exercise no legislative authority." And as far as the United States are concerned, it is proper to add, the Nineteenth Amendment to the Constitution has ended that myth. Over three centuries ago, however, Suárez, speaking of the exclusion of women, and of men below the age of twenty-five, declared in words which can not be too often quoted, as they do him infinite credit: "Some would exclude women entirely, on the ground that they can exercise no legislative authority. Among men, they exclude all below the age of twenty-five years. However, I cannot find any basis in law or any justification"—mark the words—"in reason for the exclusion of the last two groups." Francisco Suárez is rightly considered as a great theologian and philosopher, and a no less great jurist, and these qualities his various works demonstrate beyond the possibility of successful contradiction, but in the quotation which we have just made of his exact language, Suárez proclaims himself as a feminist in a day when feminism was hardly a dream, let alone a hope.

In his discussion of the state, which we do not dwell upon in this connection, it may be observed that Suárez is the outspoken advocate of consent in law, law being made with the consent of the people when it is not directly made by them. Here, however, is a short passage, which may be considered as a résumé of the doctrine applying to custom. After saying that custom can only exist through a succession of actions, he then gives as a reason that "the custom in question requires the consent of the people, and of the Prince"; and he adds that "such a multiplication of actions will be held sufficient as will make known the consent of the people"—mark again the

words, for Suárez is even today the formidable advocate of government by compact—"and the tacit approval of the Prince."

If the contention of Suárez be correct that it is only the people, and a majority of them, who can make custom, it follows necessarily that a single individual can not make custom, even though he be a judge, for a judge is authorized not to make, but to declare and apply law. The matter is of such interest, owing to the widespread objection and opposition to judge-made law, that the language of Suárez on this point is more than ordinarily important. "If the judge," he says, "rendering the opinion is not a sovereign Prince, and so does not possess legislative authority, his decision, even if it is given more than once, or if it is repeated by different judges of the same rank, does not, on the mere ground of the number of acts performed, have the effect of making law."

In law made by custom, as in all kinds of law, there must be a standard, and the standard is that the custom be founded in reason and not in error. "For if it has been established through error," Suárez says, then it would follow that, "upon discovery of the error, there disappears the apparent reason which might justify such a custom." What, then, is the consequence? "The custom itself lapses also, because it cannot exist without reason." And then follow within a modest compass further examples of what may be termed Suárez' "purple patches": "Wherefore, even though the custom will seem to stand and to establish law before the error is detected, it will do so only from an erroneous conscience; for when the truth is known, the force of the custom vanishes. It was never, therefore, true law, but merely thought to be such; and the same is true of the custom itself."

Suárez now passes from error in fact to error in law, in its effect on custom, and here again he must be allowed to speak for himself. "An error in law," he says, not less than an error of fact, "removes the element of consent in the establishment of law. For in those customs which in no way touch existing law, there can be no error as to law, save by the misapprehension that their subject-matter is either forbidden or enjoined."

There is a further passage, in which Suárez lets himself go, if such an expression be permissible in the case of so distinguished a person:

I shall say no more than that there is a much stronger reason why in the case of custom fear should be a bar to validity: and that the reason is that for a custom mere actions are not sufficient; it is essential that those actions be performed with the intention of introducing custom, which intention is commonly tacit rather than expressed. But when the actions are done solely from fear—when they would not be done except under its compulsion—they lack that intention; nor can such an intention be morally presumed, since the fear in itself, in a certain way, excludes it. Thus a frequency of actions done solely through fear, is never a sufficient evidence of the public consent of a whole people to the establishment of a custom. There is the additional consideration that the Prince cannot be presumed in such a situation to give his consent, since he does not manifest a will that his subjects be forced to adopt customs of that kind under unjust fear. And if he himself brings force and fear to bear [upon his people], he commits an injury, since he has no right to wring from his people a consent by which they are to be bound. . . .

However broad a legal custom may be according to the classification which Suárez has made, the purpose and result of such a custom are to establish law where there was no law before, in contradistinction to the custom of fact; however "not every unwritten law," Suárez points out, "is a law of custom" but only that which "has its origin in the customs and usages of a people." There might, as he says, be unwritten law established by the Prince, or by another executive—such as an officer of the Church—and subsequently it might continue to be observed "solely through the usage and tradition of his subjects." Herein lies the distinction between tradition and custom, and herein again we come upon a "purple patch," in which Suárez reiterates his faith in people and their government:

. . . For a legal custom proceeds either from a free people, and hence, one having supreme power, and, therefore, the power of enacting law; or, from one having a Pastor or Prince by whom it is governed.   In this latter case, if a legal custom is thought of—as it should be—as proceeding not from a people apart from its sovereign but from the people jointly with its Prince, that is, a people that shares in some sufficient way in the legislative power of the Prince, either by possession of the power to make its own municipal laws or statutes, or by the approval of custom, whether this approval be made manifest by law itself or declared through tacit will: a custom, I say, proceeding from a people so united with its superior, proceeds from one in which clearly the power of legislation resides. . . . It is to the will of the people that the Prince (so to speak) conforms himself, by granting the people permission, as it were, to introduce such legal custom as it may wish; or, by approving of the popular intention, or confirming it.

What a pity that the views of Suárez did not prevail in his day and generation! Yet what a blessing it is that these views—although not through Suárez—are today as commonplaces in every civilized country of the world.

In a previous passage Suárez had referred, although not in detail, to the element of intention in voluntary custom, for, in his view custom, to establish law, must not only be voluntary but must conform to the intention of those by whom it was established; and the evidence of this will and intention of the people and of the obligation which springs from this custom and to which they must, in his view, consent, is, he says, "the custom of fact itself," that is to say, the series of actions by which the customary law is established; in a word, the evidence of the legal custom is the fact of the custom.

There are other means which are and should be used in testing the validity of custom.   There is the test of reason, and the test of "sufficient usage." If a custom is in conformity with reason and if it has been established for an adequate period of time, we may safely assume that it is conducive to the public welfare and therefore that it should have "the binding power of law." The test of reason is an inherent and therefore a natural test, whereas the test of time is, we may say, artificial in that it is wholly arbitrary.   The question which needs consideration here, then, is: what is an adequate period of time?   The answer of Suárez is based on the authority of "prudent

men," who, he says, "realizing this need, hold that a period of ten years is sufficient" for the establishment of a legal custom.   Suppose, however, that the prince should not be in the country during this period or during a part of it?   His absence would not affect the matter, for Suárez maintains that the ten-year period would suffice, irrespective of the presence or absence of the Prince.   For, after all, the custom is that of the people, not of the ruler, and, while the latter might give his consent to custom if he were present in the country or even seek to oppose it, the mere continued usage over an adequate period of time, by the people, who are themselves the source of power, is sufficient.

In the case of a custom as to which there may be a doubt, there are, Suárez says, four criteria.   If the custom be "of long standing"—Suárez has just referred to the period of ten years—and is in the interest of "the general welfare, and imposes . . . a burden"—in other words, a duty, which assuredly would not be imposed if the people were not in favor of the custom—or if the observance of the custom is by "the major part of the people," then "we have," Suárez says, "sound evidence that the custom has been introduced out of a deliberate desire for the obligation that is established" or is being established by it.   This is the first criterion.

The second is enlightened public opinion—that of "prudent and God-fearing men."   If such men think ill of those who violate the custom, "or if the people generally are scandalized" at its non-observance, again "we have," Suárez says, "another strong indication of an intention on the part of the people to introduce customary law."

The third criterion concerns not the people but their prelates and governors, who, if they "gravely censure and punish those who do not follow the custom," thus supply "another important token of the binding character of the custom."

And "fourthly" and finally—and this is the supreme criterion—if the subject-matter with which the custom deals is so advantageous to the community as to make it essential for the public welfare that the custom be binding, then any doubt concerning it is disposed of: clearly the custom has been introduced for the good of the people.   For the all-inclusive test of law, whether it be written or customary, is, after all, that the subject-matter of each and every variety be "morally sound, adapted to the public good, and, finally, reasonable"; for "reason," Suárez finely and impressively says, "is, as it were, the soul of both kinds of law."

It need not be said that Suárez has shown himself to be a consummate jurist and master in the legal forum.   But he was also a churchman, and the forum of conscience was never absent from his thoughts.   And if the written law is to be moral and its morality tested by conscience, so should custom be binding in conscience, for it is law—indeed, he expressly says in this passage, "it is true law"—and the obligation of customary law is, he adds, to be "judged" precisely as in the case of the written law, "according

to the character of the subject-matter," if the will of the people has not otherwise provided.

There is therefore a sanction in the forum of conscience. Can custom provide a material sanction? The answer of Suárez is in the affirmative, to the effect that there may be a penal sanction, "for," he says, "what absurdity in reason can be shown in the possibility of a custom binding under a physical penalty as well as under the moral one of the stain of guilt?"

After having discussed the question of the abrogation of custom by law, Suárez reverses the question and asks whether a law may be abrogated by custom. His answer is in the affirmative; for the authority to abolish law, as well as to make law, is primarily in the people, and if through them a custom is established which is contrary to a given law, the law falls before the will of the people. The exercise of this power, however, is usually through the government which the people have established, and this power, Suárez says, "must be explained as resulting from a union of the people with their Prince and lawmaker," the reason being, Suárez adds, "that this power to put aside a law, as it exists in the people taken alone, is rather a factual than a legal one." The rôle which the prince plays in the matter is, we might say, that of a silent partner, who supplies the legal formalities and has the "power to tolerate and give consent to the popular will."

Now, whether the people make their laws directly or whether they have delegated their powers of lawmaking to their representatives, the effect is the same so far as the abolition of laws by custom is concerned. It is sufficient, as Suárez observes, "that they have a capacity for law," and that the custom which is to abrogate the law should "be introduced by those to whom the law is to apply." The reason for this is that the repudiation of a law is not a matter of jurisdiction on the part of those in power nor is it a matter of the public authority which they exercise. It is "rather one that proceeds from those under a duty of obedience to the law," that is to say, a law should be repudiated only by those to whom it applies, and not by those who execute it.

A custom contrary to a law introduced by the people does not "actively," as Suárez says, abolish law. Rather the custom is the voice of the people demanding that "the superior . . . abolish the law." And woe betide him if he is deaf to the voice of his fellow-countrymen! The action of the people, therefore, is, as Suárez puts it, the manifestation of "an intention not to have or retain the law in question, or"—again in the language of this champion of liberty—"to resume the earlier status of freedom from legal obligation" in the matter in hand. And the intention itself, he concludes, "is sufficiently manifest from the agreement and constancy of the people in actions to that end"; for custom, does it not spring from the agreement and constancy of the people in action?

We now come upon a passage in which Suárez anticipates—unconsciously, of course—the action of the people of the United States in regard to

the Eighteenth Amendment to the Constitution of the United States, forbidding the manufacture and sale of intoxicating liquors. His language
here is, if we may say so, in point:

From a public custom made up of actions in violation of law, especially from such a custom
when it is tolerated, there results such an ignorance of the law that the offense comes to be
regarded as less serious; or, if not ignorance of the law, such an insensitiveness to the un-
lawfulness of the act, is induced as lessens the gravity of the fault, and, consequently, of the
liability to punishment.

Indeed we might here rest the case in behalf of customs made up of
actions in violation of law; but Suárez felt the matter to be—as do we of the
United States—of more than passing importance.   Therefore he adds:

The example of the violation of the law by great numbers of people presents a very strong
temptation, as it were, drawing the violator on by a vehement desire and passion; and this
fact must usually be accounted as a mitigating circumstance in individual violations of the
law.

As we are inditing these lines, the Supreme Court of the United States has
rendered a decision which in effect has quashed some thirteen thousand suits
for violations of the law, on the ground that the Eighteenth Amendment
itself having been repealed, there is no liability after repeal for its violation,
although the violation in question took place while the Eighteenth Amendment was still in effect.[1]   This would seem to be a concession to "vehement
desire and passion."   In delivering the opinion of the Supreme Court, Mr.
Chief Justice Hughes expressed in stately and unforgettable language the
fundamental conception of the Spanish School that the source of power is
vested in the people.   "The question," in the language of the learned Chief
Justice, "is not one of public policy which the courts may be considered free
to declare, but of the continued efficacy of legislation in the face of controlling
action of the people, the source of the power to enact and maintain it.   It is
not a question of the developing common law. . . . Prosecution for crimes
is but an application or enforcement of the law, and if the prosecution continues the law must continue to vivify it.   The law, here sought to be
applied, was deprived of force by the people themselves as the inescapable
effect of their repeal of the Eighteenth Amendment.   The principle involved
is thus not archaic but rather is continuing and vital,—that the people are
free to withdraw the authority they have conferred and, when withdrawn,
neither the Congress nor the courts can assume the right to continue to
exercise it."

And, because of its unfortunate appositeness to present conditions in our
beloved country, we again invoke Suárez: "With respect to the community
in general, the multitude of offenders gives rise to the occasion for a lapse in
the execution of the penalty, for the reason that it is not easy to punish so
large a number without scandal, or without causing great disorder and very
serious harm to the community.   Neither is it expedient to punish some,

[1] *United States* v. *Chambers et al.*, 291 U. S. 217, 226 (1934).

and not others, since this also would give rise to scandal through charges of favoritism.   Even when punishment can, for a particular reason, be visited upon some persons, these are usually few in number, and immunity is the rule with the generality of the people."   It is with a deep sense of humiliation that we mention a form of violation of law in these United States—a violation so often unpunished, that it has almost come to have the power of customary law and which bears the opprobrious title of "lynch law."

Without quoting the maxim *Cessante ratione legis, cessat ipsa lex*, Suárez compresses within three paragraphs the entire philosophy of the cessation of custom:

If . . . the matter is so changed that the reason and end of the custom disappear, not only in some particular respects, but in general, then the obligation of the custom will lapse also.

Indeed, should the change in circumstances be such that the purpose for which the custom was introduced does not so much disappear as work to vicious effect, then there may be a positive duty not to observe the custom.   This would be the case should the custom begin to be a moral occasion of sin, or be otherwise harmful to the general good of the commonwealth.   The same will be true, if, in some particular case, the reason for the custom not only ceases simply to be, but produces opposite effects.   This principle we have shown to be true of written law, and it is equally applicable to custom.

Finally it is clear that this is the only way in which custom can of itself cease to exist; since it is not dependent upon any other cause as an active principle to preserve it, as it were, in being.   For although the custom may depend upon the will of the sovereign, the fact that he does not revoke it is enough for its preservation; and the same is true also of the popular will, in so far as the custom is dependent upon it.

* * *

It was to be expected that Suárez contemplated a sanction for each of the various kinds of laws with which he has dealt.   It might, however, be a sanction differing from that of Victoria, because Victoria was dealing with law in a specific and concrete case.   Now Victoria stated the sanction by implication, if not in unmistakable and incontrovertible terms, the sanction resting upon the natural authority of the state, by appropriate legislation, to protect all human beings within its jurisdiction—whether in their individual or in their united capacity—in the enjoyment of their rights and the performance of their duties under the law of nations; and, failing to do so— failing, that is, in its duty, both national and international, and in what we of today call "due diligence"—the state was to be liable, before the international community, in damages for such negligence.[1]

---

[1] *De Jure Belli*, sections 19, 41, Carnegie Institution edition above cited, pp. 172–3, 181: . . . princes have authority not only over their own subjects, but also over foreigners, so far as to prevent them from committing wrongs, and this is by the law of nations and by the authority of the whole world.   Nay, it seems to be by natural law also, seeing that otherwise society could not hold together unless there was somewhere a power and authority to deter wrongdoers and prevent them from injuring the good and innocent.   Now, everything needed for the government and preservation of society exists by natural law, and in no other way can we show that a State has by natural law authority to inflict pains and penalties on its citizens who are dangerous to it. . . .

. . . For instance, if French brigands made a raid into Spanish territory and the French King would not, though able, compel them to restore their booty, the Spanish might on

The difference between Victoria and Suárez is that Victoria stated the sanction as a fact and Suárez states it as a philosophy.

Suárez was dealing with law in general as well as with law in its several branches. It was therefore natural that he should contemplate a sanction which would be general in its nature, instead of specific. That sanction was to be for him as a first principle. And the natural law being the basis of his system, the sanction was therefore rooted in the natural law.

The natural law being universal, the sanction would also be universal; otherwise there would not be a complete sanction for the law natural. If there be a right and if there be a duty under the law natural, the sanction protecting the right and enforcing the duty should, like the law, be natural. Now the obligation under a rule of law, whether it deal with the law natural, civil law, or the law international, was assimilated by Suárez to the natural law. The reason? That good faith is a natural principle, and in his conception an obligation under any category of law would be incomplete unless the obligation were executed in good faith. Therefore, with Suárez, the obligation to execute a human compact or agreement made under any form of law was a *natural* obligation, requiring compliance of the state or the community through a municipal statute or, as we would say, a municipal sanction.

This conception is vastly important, so important that it must be considered in all it various implications. So far as temporal things are concerned—for we are not dealing in this connection with the divine law as such —the natural law is, in Suárez' conception, the fundamental law underlying all man-made law. It is the law conformable and conforming to human nature and, we would add, to the dignity of the human being, as such; and as human beings are scattered throughout the world, it is a universal law. Now good faith is an inherent element—indeed, the essence—of the natural law, and therefore any and every obligation, whether it arises from the natural law itself or, through intervention of the human being, from the law of the state or from that of the international community, is *natural* in the sense that its execution is required by good faith. Hence, in the system of Suárez, the obligation, however it arises, flows directly from the natural law, or indirectly from the natural law through the law of the state or the law of the states, and is thus a natural obligation.

There is here, however, a further observation to be made. If the obligation belongs to the natural law, the legislation to carry it into effect is either of the states individually or of the states collectively as they form the international community. In other words, the obligation in essence is one of good faith; its execution is a thing separate and distinct, the latter being

the authorization of their sovereign, despoil French merchants or farmers, however innocent these might be. This is because, although the French State or sovereign might initially be blameless, yet it is a breach of duty, as St. Augustine says, for them to neglect to vindicate the right against the wrongdoing of their subjects, and the injured sovereign can take satisfaction from every member and portion of their State. . . .

municipal and requiring municipal action whether the obligation be national or international. In short, the obligation is one thing, the execution is another thing, but together they are natural law in action.

To approach the matter from another angle and, by what may seem a restatement, to clear up any possible misconception, the obligation, when created, becomes an obligation of natural law, and, as every obligation is thus an integral part of the natural law, it should be carried out in good faith—which is an all-pervading principle of the natural law. Hence it is the inescapable duty of every state under the law of nature to supply the appropriate measure or means for carrying into effect the obligation; thus, for example, it is universally a duty to execute any and every agreement properly entered into in good faith. If the agreement is made within the state, the obligation, like the law to enforce its execution, is national. If the agreement is between states, the obligation is international, separate and distinct from the statutory or municipal law which may be necessary to carry it into effect. And here we catch, as it were, a glimpse of the sanction, in the form of a municipal statute, *in esse* or *in posse*, to carry into effect an international pact or agreement creating an obligation under the law of nature.

Why should "a pact and agreement," to quote Victoria, require a sanction? Because the conception of a universal law controlling human beings in all their actions would be imperfect if the obligation imposed upon human beings were not to be executed, since the law universal would then be but a series of precepts in the abstract; it would not be precepts in action. And the precept in action requires a municipal sanction to carry it into effect. Whether the obligation arises from a contract between two or more individuals, whether it be a compact of groups of individuals or whether it be that most formal of agreements known as a treaty or convention, to which all of the states of the world may be parties in an international conference, the natural element of good faith pervades each and every one and requires the execution of the obligation. Although we as yet have no international legislature, nevertheless we have and have had from time out of mind a rule of international law flowing from the natural law, and binding the groups of human beings which we are pleased to call states. The rule is a Latin maxim, *Pacta sunt servanda.*

We have the precept and the obligation to carry it into effect; the one without the other is incomplete. It is therefore the manifest duty of every community to provide the sanction by which good faith in all human legal relations is observed, whether these relations be between individual and individual, between individual and community, or between state and state—in a word, however they may arise.

There can be no association of human beings except upon a moral basis, because man is a moral animal; and the first, indeed the greatest, of the foundations of human society is good faith. How can people associate

except on terms of good faith? And good faith, is it not the prime natural principle in the relationship of human beings?

As man is a moral being he differs, we are prone to think, from the brute creation in that he possesses a conscience. The conscience of man is an individual thing; the conscience of nations, if the expression be permissible, is enlightened public opinion. And public opinion is, or must be in the long run, moral opinion, for it is but the expression of the collective conscience of moral and human beings.

This is Suárez' philosophic demonstration of the Victorian sanction.

In the conception of Suárez there is no rule of law which does not create a natural obligation, whether the immediate transaction out of which the obligation arises be between individuals, between individuals and states, or between state and state. Put, then, in terms of the lawyer, there is no rule of law, national or international, which does not create a natural duty and a legal obligation, and, if legislation on the part of a state does not enforce and render that obligation effective by providing the means to carry it out, the state itself is recreant in its duty.

To repeat, there is no rule of law without a legal obligation, the obligation being a consequence of law, and made explicit by the statute which creates it; but although the obligation is, as it were, the creature of statute, its ultimate source is the natural law and the duty to put it into effect carries with it the further duty to display due diligence in its execution—duties which arise from the natural principle of good faith, present in the heart and conscience of every human being.

Indeed, to violate good faith is to violate the moral law, which is, in essence, the law of nature "written in the heart of man," as it were, "with the finger of God."